FIND YOUR VOICE

The Life You Crave is
a Conversation Away

FIND YOUR VOICE

Book Cover & Interior Design by Monkey C Media
www.MonkeyCMedia.com

Printed in the United States of America

BBL Publishing
An imprint of Build.Buzz.Launch. Media
8718 Redondo Drive, Dallas, TX 75218

ISBNs:
978-0-9909725-2-5 (paperback)
978-0-9909-725-3-2 (ebook)

Dedicated to Mom, Marisa, and Beed.
Thank you for your love, understanding,
and for giving my voice room to grow.

I love you.

TABLE OF CONTENTS

My Journey...

Your Voice...

INTRODUCTION

What were you just thinking?

Can you remember the thoughts that motivated you to pick up this book?

That's the voice you will find, get to know, and own as yours through these pages.

That voice is yourbirthright.

She holds great wisdom, love, solutions, creativity, courage, and nurturing.
She can also speak anxiety, depression, embarrassment, perfectionism, and worry.

Your voice is your story.
Your voice is your perspective.
Are you the victim or the heroine?
Finding your voice gives you the choice.

She (your inner voice) translates your world from the moment you rise.
Sometimes she keeps you up at night.

She helps you communicate and share with others.
She decides to keep or free your heart and creativity.
She gives you strength and solutions in the face of challenging times.
She can also talk you right out of a brave move if she is stuck in the past.
She is in there, forming your life.

Her words influence your emotions and then your actions.

Although she is with you all the time, you may not be aware of the tone of her voice or remember to rebut her unhealthy decisions before they turn to action.

Our backgrounds are probably nothing alike, and that doesn't matter.

You and I are both women living, giving, and thriving in this world.

We have both gone through experiences, big and small, that have stayed with us and dimmed or muted the full power of our voices.

One of the most authentic voices we have as women is our nature to nurture. It can be motherhood or just holding great empathy for a dear friend or stranger.

Adopting the voice of permission will be one of your greatest achievements in finding your voice.

With that voice you will learn to **give** to yourself.

Give yourself permission to…

…listen

…take leaps

…not be perfect

…set boundaries

…make mistakes

…let go of control

…feel the range of your emotions

…stop constantly comparing yourself

…speak up against your negative voice

…offer credibility to your most powerful voice

…take care of your well-being without feeling guilty

…know who you are in the face of a compliment or critique

…get to know the tone of your voice and actively participate with it

I share with you my stories, not for you to find similarity in the time, place, or scenery, but for you to know **you are not alone** in the emotions that are left with you.

You are not the only one who feels lost, unheard, anxious, incapable, unlovable, full of regret, shamed, hopeless, pressured to be perfect, compelled to control, low in your worth, stuck, and scared of your future.

We rarely give a voice to the emotions that are socially unacceptable or hard to deal with.

Finding your voice will give you the courage and patience to sit and hear your emotions with no judgment.

This offers you a great tool to stay graceful in the face of challenging times. Which are inevitable.

I also share my stories with you because I want you to succeed.

It's a process to find your voice. There are stages and layers that I will guide you through so you will be more cognizant of her.

I want you to adopt a realistic voice for yourself and your process.

This book is not something else that you should feel bad about.

Know that your process may feel like one *a-ha* moment after another. It can also take you away from these pages for days, maybe weeks. You will come back once you are ready to explore the next layer of your inner voice.

If you're making excuses to not go through this process even though your voice needs it, you will feel guilt or sadness. This is a crucial opportunity to find YOUR voice and pick up this book again.

The yearning feeling that led you here will not go away until your voice is heard.

Whatever voice you have adopted has most likely been with you for a while. For you to overcome your old perspective and trust the power of your own voice, you will have to respect your unique timeline.

This is the space where you will learn the relationship between your inner voice, your emotions, and the life that forms from them. I am here to support you and there are plenty of resources for you at www.FindYourVoice.center.

READER & GROUP GUIDE

I invite you to use this book like your journal. This is not a book to pass on to another friend. This is a safe place to bare it all.

You get to write all over these pages. Random words and streams of consciousness. The surface and core of you.

You get to come back and see what you've written. You get to read your perspective. You get to see how you've grown and have a blueprint for how to pick yourself up when challenges arise. Again and again. Faster and faster.

Finding your voice is a lifelong process in some ways. The fact that you've picked up this book lets me know that you are a woman who is conscious of herself and is willing to work towards change.

That quality will stay with you for the rest of your life.

Celebrate that. It also means you will continue to challenge yourself to grow.

Each chapter starts with a story that reflects a poignant experience in my life that repeated itself in my head for years.

As you read my story, reflect on your own. Start with the present day. Do not feel overwhelmed by trying to dig down too far.

Each chapter offers written conversation and physical exercises to help with where you are in the process of this book.

Having a support system is huge. There is not one woman whose perspective roots for her all the time.

Finding your voice is keeping your grace and knowing your worth during these difficult times. Invite a friend, sister, cousin, or virtual gal pal to go through this process with you.

The more positive voices you have in your life, the easier it will be to fine-tune your voice.

If you've partnered with one or more people for this process, here are some really simple guidelines to facilitate your meetings.

~Keep it real. Our schedules demand a lot from us, so make a realistic schedule when it comes to meeting up with each other. Take into account all the technology at your fingertips and use Facetime, Google Hangout, Skype, or just a good ol' phone call.

~Decide how often you want to meet, keep it the same every month, and get creative with it! Maybe you meet in person once a month and schedule 1 to 2 fifteen-minute phone calls and supportive texts in between!

~Set a start and end time. Setting a specific amount of time will help you divide the time evenly so that each person has the same amount of time to speak. I also suggest allowing a slot of time for feedback and support after each person speaks.

~What's on the agenda. There are questions to be answered in every chapter. You can let these be your guide or see what else comes up organically. Sometimes you just need to apply this entire process to one area of your life or one goal. Let each person decide what she wants to share. You don't have to share the same thing because each of you will have a different process.

Let's say I have a group of 3 and we've dedicated 60 minutes to our Find Your Voice (chapter 1). We're going over the first set of questions. Here's how we might split up our time:

- 10 minutes – Hey girl! How you doin'? Everyone gets to catch up.
- 10 minutes – *Samantha, we're all ears, girl! It's your turn to use your voice.*
- 5 minutes – group gives *Samantha* support/feedback
- 10 minutes – *Amy, we're all ears, girl! It's your turn to use your voice.*
- 5 minutes – group gives *Amy* support/feedback
- 10 minutes – *Bianca, we're all ears, girl! It's your turn to use your voice.*
- 5 minutes – group gives *Bianca* support/feedback
- 10 minutes extra left for transition time & wrap up.

~Support & Feedback. During this time, help each other **define one specific goal** to walk away with and to hold each other accountable for until your next meeting.

This is when I love texting! I am busy and so is my friend, but I want to check on her to see if she made that phone call, or wrote that e-mail, or kept her promise of going to the gym or a dance class. So I shoot her a quick text to check in. It's as easy as that.

One

THE SHUSHED VOICE

RED SHOES

SPRING 1984 ~ TEHRAN, IRAN ~ FOOROSHGHA BOZORG

Tak tak tak tak

That's the rhythm of happiness. The noise and repetition that let me know I actually exist.

That there is a space that my body occupies; it has weight, and this is what it sounds like in half-inch red patent heels.

Tak tak tak tak

I begged my Mom for the "*tak tak* shoes" for two weeks after seeing them in the window of Foorooshgha Bozorg (Grand Market).

She had never seen me so persistent. As a result of my courage to ask, and commitment to do so repeatedly, she gave in and bought them for me.

I remember my chest feeling light and fluttery as we walked through the bazaar to buy my beloved shoes. When we got there I eyed the selection of mini heels. The shape and color didn't seem to matter much. It was the sound the heel made with every step that I was most concerned with.

I tried on a pretty red pair of Mary Janes—the glossy, cherry-red that little girls favor—but the click of the heel did not please my ears at all.

It was a pair of deep red, round-toe, half-inch heels that made the loudest **tak** that became the object of my adoration for the next eight months.

I wanted to be heard. The soles of my feet did what my young soul could not do.

I wore them from the moment I woke up in my pajamas, and they remained on my feet all day, sometimes outlasting the four or five outfits I had to change into for my solo tea parties.

When it was time to go to bed, I would beg my mom to let me sleep with them on. We reached an agreement that I could sleep with them next to me.

I eventually outgrew my heels, but still insisted on squeezing into them. It was the law, not my mom, that eventually stopped me.

My childhood version of the fashion police was the Islamic authorities who wore AK-47s and clubs like statement necklaces.

My mom's floral scarf, which lay decoratively on her head in Parisian style, changed to a thick black *chador (a big scarf that covers everything except the face),* covering her head-to-toe. Far from being Parisian, far from being Persian, but clearly the symbol of the new Islamic Republic of Iran.

I still chose beautiful outfits that my mom had sewn with bows and lace. But the joy of parading my fanciness around crumbled as I pulled over my *magnae* and *rupush (magnae covers from head to below the chest worn with a rupush, a thick fabric that covers body shape down to ankles and needs to be paired with black socks).*

I had two wardrobes: a colorful one full of patterns and frilly trim and another that was just gray, navy, or black to cover up any girliness.

It was so hot under all of our layers that mom cut both of our hair short, just like the Islamic police.

Steadily, the police became a prominent fixture in my everyday life, morphing from men who waved their batons in the air, to scowling women in all black, the new face of our womanly identities.

Walking around town, these women kept a close and judgmental eye on their peers and scolded them if hair was showing or their makeup was too alluring. There were stories whispered from one woman to another about jail time and even stoning for those who resisted.

It was shameful to attract any attention to yourself as a woman. If you were beautiful, had an opinion, or said something smart and someone noticed—God forbid, a man—it was your fault for arousing any attention. SHAME on you. It was made law for us to be invisible.

A wave of fear began to drown the women in my life.

Their hands, once adorned by gold rings and nail polish, now pale and shameful, would grab their chador, pinching the fabric tight underneath their chin at the sight of an officer. Suffocating anything left of their womanhood.

The sidewalk and its people had never monopolized my focus this way before; it was usually the colorful clothes and sparkling gold jewelry in store windows that I would gawk at.

Now, I walked by the same shoe store and didn't even bother looking in. The veil of sadness began to cover me. Even the fantasies of a 7-year-old girl became impossible.

The fluttering joy in my heart had flown away. I became quiet. My chest became heavy from holding all the emotions that surrounded me. The muscles in my face became too heavy for any expression, especially a smile.

Soon after, the fluttering in my chest would return, at a sporadic and uneasy rhythm, and my life would be changed forever.

There was an invisible anger that filled my house. I never got to see it, but I could hear it, sometimes, and I always felt it between my parents.

The thunder of my dad's voice was nothing compared to the shrieking sirens that woke us up nightly.

The war between Iran and Iraq was no longer reserved for the borders. Tehran and its citizens were now the main target.

In a hushed stampede we would leave our apartment, stop one floor down to fetch my grandparents, and continue to shuffle down to the basement, waiting for the ultimate tremble.

The trembles that would light up the black of the night.
The bass that would shake our bodies and our buildings.
The songs of bombs that would paint the town what used to be my favorite color—red.

The thoughts of what I would wake up to the next day always kept me up far later than the bombs did.

It always took me a long time to wake up to the reality of the day, long after the opening of my eyelids. Heavy in my face, my burdensome body dragging along, I would walk to our living room window and look down onto the street to see how my walk to school had changed, again.

After eyeing the sidewalk for new cracks, gaps, and piles of concrete, I walked to the far left end of the couch, pressed my left cheek into the window as much as I could, forcing the round flesh between my teeth. Closing my right eye and squinting the left, I could focus on my friend's building.

Relief. It was still there.

I dragged my feet as I went down the hallway, back to my room to once again put on the layers of darkness that muted my already shushed existence.

THE SHUSHED VOICE

*T*he nearly eight years I lived in Iran instilled the voice of shame within me, and I had no idea.

This voice of shame would turn into the voice of perfectionism once I immigrated to the States. Eventually, the voice would lead me to planning my own death and half a year in different psych wards.

I have journals that span the majority of my life. Although I wrote in them regularly, I would not go back and read them. I was constantly pushing back who I was with regret.

Journal after journal.
Year after year.
Milestone after milestone.

I interpreted my life, even in times of success, with shuddering remorse. This left me operating from the same space, journal after journal, year after year.

I adopted the perspective of what I felt growing up—there is no value in my existence. I avoided reflecting on my journals for this very reason.

No matter what successes I recorded, it was not enough. I was not enough.

Unable to form a relationship with my inner voice, my body, mind, and bank account grew, while my value, my perspective, was that of a shushed girl who needed love and validation.

I shared with you the beginning of my journey because the invisible, sad girl you just met is who I stayed until I was 25. Her voice guided my decisions until then.

I am sharing the entire process of losing and finding my voice for you to see it is a **process,** as is your existence. You cannot fight the passing of time and the challenges that come with it.

You can, however, make a choice to get to know all the voices within you, and offer them a space to be expressed.

Give permission to the voice of anxiousness, hopelessness, or perfectionism.

When they are heard, they will calm down.

When they are heard, your emotional and physical behavior will be in harmony.

When they are heard, you will be able to keep a graceful voice during challenging times.

There are stages and layers. Respect your process.

My journey to find my voice took me back to the very start; your process may not reflect the same.

Your process will lead you as far back as you need to go. This is something that will reveal itself to you far beyond the time you spend in these pages.

At this point, I hope you have not adopted a *voice of comparison* when it comes to my journey and yours.

You don't need a decade's worth of journals or a childhood as volatile as mine to have lost your voice or to now crave the full expression of your voice.

In some ways, I'm lucky. The messages that were forced on me are easily identifiable—so much so, that they are now etched in history books.

It is easy for me to be able to state what led to the start of me losing my voice, the power that is my **birthright.**

For you, the experiences or unspoken rules that took away your power could have been caused by poignant moments like mine, or in small silent expectations like…

"Be a good girl."

"Don't be pushy!"

"Don't be too loud!"

"You are too opinionated!"

"Be nice, and act like a lady!"

"Why are you acting so emotional?"

"Don't ask for a raise; you'll get one when you deserve it."

"That's a male-dominant field; maybe think of another route."

Reflect on some expectations you have adopted.

Unspoken definitions (expectations) I have for myself...

Our histories don't need to have any similarity. The fact is, we both have adopted a voice—a perspective—that does not serve us.

The voice I'm referring to is the same voice that guides you. The one that gave you a hunch that it was time for a change. What started as a single thought began to repeat, perhaps so much that you didn't hear it anymore, but you began to feel...

...frustration at feeling unheard

...restless because you want more

...a burning need to reach your potential

...sadness for the decisions you've made

...exhausted from being so hard on yourself

...tired of the anxiety that comes with perfectionism

...tired of running on empty, but guilty about caring for yourself

...ready for the commitment to adopt a long-term solution

These are the kinds of feelings that brought out an action in you. This motivation for a transformation is what brought you to this page.

You have already taken the first step by opening, reading, digesting. Now, let's begin to explore the relationship between your voice, your perspective, your emotions, and the behaviors that form your life. One word at a time. One layer at a time.

The start of finding your voice begins with where you are **at this moment.**

Look up from this page, close your eyes, allow the space between your eyes to relax, and unclench your jaw.

Listen to what's floating through your mind at this moment.

You are not looking for anything specific. Listen as short or as long as you want.

I was just thinking...

How was that for you?

Are you noticing a certain tone in your voice?

Energized? Judgmental? Tired? Sad? Anxious?

There are no right answers, and there is no right timeline.

This moment, all you need to do is **give yourself permission** to listen to yourself more.

Not in the way you need to listen to yourself, your gut, when you are toiling over a decision, but to tune in to the inner commentator that gives you the play-by-play of all your moments. Your inner voice.

Offering yourself permission to listen, then actually accepting this gesture, are **two very different voices** within you.

This concept of giving myself permission did not come to me until I was 25 and walking out the doors of my last hospital stay for yet another suicide attempt. It was 2005.

That entire year after I was released I gave myself permission to be "reborn", to start anew.

It sounds poetic, but in reality it was not.

I was 25, and most of my days were filled with appointments with therapists and psychologists, writing in mood journals, and knitting. Meanwhile, most of my friends were taking the next steps in their careers and love lives, and even talking about investing in property.

I had to give myself permission to **NOT compare** myself to my peers, the expectations for my age, or the expectations for a Persian woman. Expectations that were repeated silently by my own mind and aloud by a few family members.

I had to quietly give myself permission several times a day to listen and <u>detach</u> from the voice that would tell me I am…

> a lost f**k-up, unheard, unloveable, incapable, with no idea what to do next.

Every day for an entire year, I would write in my journal a line I learned from the one yoga class I had taken…

I am exactly where I need to be.

Respect **your** process.

Most times I would rebut the voice of permission that allowed me to become aware of these thoughts. I knew it was going to be a long road to healing, and sometimes I wanted to shove the words and pain back down and I would tell my voice of permission to *shut the hell up.*

You will find that listening to your inner voice can take you down many a winding road.

Allow yourself to hear the various thoughts that you have and practice no judgment or attachment to them. It will be difficult not to engage in a conversation with your inner voice. *I should have… Now I need to… He's such a… Why did that happen…*

Instead of judging or getting attached to your inner voice, give yourself permission to **listen to her like a third-party, a spectator, an observer.**

Your voice is already in there, all the time, doing what it does. You just need to practice listening without judgment or attachment.

You're looking for the tone of voice you take when it comes to yourself and others.

Start becoming aware of how you think and what emotions show up as a result.

Through this you'll begin to notice your emotional changes more and more. Get in the habit of asking yourself,

"What was I just thinking?"

Notice I said **practice.**

You will continue to think and act as you do, but you'll add this to your repertoire.

Do not overwhelm yourself by expecting to be attuned to every thought.

Let's do a little practicing right now. I want you to reflect on how ready you are to find your voice.

Finding your voice is much like learning a new language; it will take time, practice, and permission.

How you answer these questions will give you great insight to your process.

This is not a race. It is a process.

Respect what you write down, but also listen to what you think or visualize that you did not record. There are a lot of answers in this space.

On a scale of 1–10 how motivated are you?
1– not so much, 10– let's do this!

Which of these sounds like you:

~ *I want to change. I've thought about it. Buying this book is the first step.*

~ *I am tired of thinking about change. I want to do something more. I already have a list of goals, I'm just looking for the best approach.*

~ *I'm organized and feel clear about what I need to change. I'm ready to commit time, courageous enough to feel the emotions, and willing to make the leap.*

What will life be like when you find your voice?
Describe in words, drawings, and visualizations

What are the challenges you expect along this process?

How do you think you will deal with these challenges?

Describe a situation in your past where you were successful at change.

What will life be like if you give up and stay as you are?

Who do you have in your support system?

Do you have a spiritual practice?

Who or what is your anchor?

Did you notice that you thought one thing and wrote down something else?

There are a lot of answers in the place between your automatic voice and your most authentic voice.

This is such a sacred space.

What did you think that you did not write?

How you answered will give you a lot of insight about the process you are about to begin.

There is always a self-imposed pressure of how you should go about a goal and how motivated you should be.

I am asking you to remember that these pages are a safe place. Do not lie to yourself. Be realistic with how you work.

Don't be hard on yourself. If you feel deep down that you are scared or that you'll make a half-ass attempt, then put this book on the shelf.

If your process takes you away from finding your voice, respect that, because your need for change is still festering in your conscious, and it will reveal itself again.

You are just working through another layer. If you put this book down at this very moment, take this with you:

What was I just thinking?

If you are hard on yourself,
you will never create a space for change.

You are where you are, and that is exactly where we are going to begin.

Give yourself permission and respect.

Make a space in your life for recording your inner voice. You can use the pages of this book, you can use the downloads at www.FindYourVoice.center, or you can use a notes page in your smartphone.

You may use all of the above, depending on your lifestyle and process.

Journal as much as you can throughout this process. It's okay if you are not much of a writer. Random thoughts, doodles, and drawings are all welcome. They all represent your inner voice.

Begin to record what's floating in your conscious at the start and end of your day. You don't have to write an essay or even a complete sentence. Make this a doable task. If all you have is a sleepy five minutes, take advantage—just get started.

Morning voice...

Evening voice...

It's great to stay conscious of what you're thinking throughout the day; however, we think so many thoughts that this can be overwhelming.

Instead, I encourage you to notice when your mood changes, and then ask yourself...

What was I just thinking?

Understanding the voice you adopt in emotional times is such a gift. I encourage you to keep a mood chart to begin to see the link between your inner voice and your life.

Physical Reaction...	Behavior...	Feeling...	Thought...

It doesn't matter what you believe in, there is a beautiful correlation between listening to your own voice and putting your trust in the intangible, the invisible—the spiritual.

My first interaction with religion was more like a set of laws than a spiritual support system. But once I started a spiritual conversation, I was able to trust my own voice.

Through relying on your spiritual support system, you will build more of a relationship with the voice you are meant to have.

Your creator intended you to have **a voice of your own. It is your birthright.**

Tuning into the quiet space between your thoughts, which often comes as a result of a spiritual practice, is a wonderful way to get in touch with your voice.

As important as it is to know what's in your head, it's very important to get out of it sometimes.

Regardless of your faith, I encourage you to meditate. To quiet your mind.

Meditation can be a very intimidating thing. I always encourage those who are frightened by it to start with meditation in motion. Yoga and walking are wonderful activities that allow you to practice not being attached to your thoughts. When thoughts come up, practice letting them float by and the space between your thoughts **will** get longer and longer.

If this gets increasingly difficult for you, pick one word for your inhale and another for your exhale. Don't be frustrated when your other thoughts interrupt; keep going back to your intention. You are strengthening your voice by doing this.

I have also created a meditation specific for this journey at www.FindYourVoice.center.

HEAR. HERE.

Vehicle for release

Write the words that are serving as your blocks.

Observe

How have your emotions changed due to these thoughts?

I

How will you give yourself permission to be released from this perspective?

Challenge

Challenge your negative voice here.

Embrace

How can you embrace this part of your process?

Keep asking yourself...

What was I just thinking?

TWO

ABANDONED VOICE

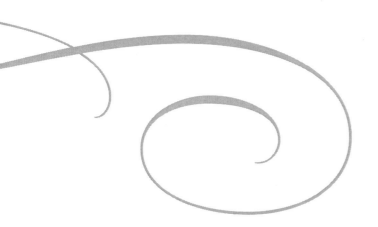

LAND OF THE FREE

SUMMER 1986 ~ DENVER, COLORADO ~ STAPLETON AIRPORT

A month after our arrival in America—land of the free—I was back at the airport. I grabbed my roller skates off the x-ray belt at Stapleton Airport and laced them back up.

We were living with my uncle and his American wife and daughter in Denver now.

I had traded in my chador for roller skates.

I was told to stop talking Farsi and start watching *One Life To Live*.

I replaced the sounds of bombs for WHAM and Michael Jackson cassette tapes.

I was no longer called *Sahar* by my classmates, but *Terrorist or Bomb Keeper;* on a good day I would be called *Sarah*.

And now, I would have to find a replacement for the affection of my father.

We had brought my father here to fly back to Iran to gather the remainder of our belongings, but I knew at just 10 years old that this would be his departure from my life.

We stopped by his gate. I couldn't sit still. I didn't want to say goodbye to another part of my life or watch my estranged parents coldly part ways. Instead, I roamed in circles, feeling the give-and-take of my wheels rolling between carpet and tile.

When it was time for the big goodbye he casually called me over. Kneeling down, he hugged me, then my brother, with no extra effort. Like any other day, he just said goodbye and walked through the gate.

My mom, brother, and I stood and watched him disappear around the corner and out of our lives.

I looked up at my mom's pale, blank face and wondered how she felt. After all her efforts to get us here, he didn't even stay a full season to help us build our new life.

Mom and I understood the finality of this moment. My brother, too young to translate what was happening, thought our father worked on a plane for the next year.

I felt detached on our way home from the airport. What had been a heaviness in my body began to feel floaty.

My uncle's Subaru had a sunroof. I knew once we hit 6th Avenue I would be able to stand up and stick my head out and get away from these feelings.

My Iranian boy hair cut was growing out and I could feel strands of my hair whipping across my face as I emerged from the sunroof.

The sting it left on my skin was a slight distraction from the fire of anger that was rising within me. A feeling that would overtake my body and force my spirit out. When I couldn't stand the sensation of heaviness and pain, I would begin to watch my life from outside of my body.

SPRING 1992 ~ DENVER, COLORADO ~ MY ROOM

*M*mmmmmmmmmmmmhhe," A low angry vibration filled my chest as I threw clothes from the pile at the bottom of my closet.

I was in my neon floral skirt and training bra, looking for my loose-fitting black tee shirt. I loved to roll up its sleeves and wear it with my spandex skirt like Kelly on *Saved By The Bell.*

"Finally!" I threw it on and headed to my last day of school.

I walked to school among the trees of the greenbelt like I always did, waiting for beams of sun to peek through the branches and warm me up.

I couldn't get used to the stark difference in temperature from morning to afternoon, and this morning I refused to wear any extra layers.

"It's almost summer. I hate Denver," I mumbled under my breath.

I folded my arms and tucked in my chin to preserve my body heat, when I noticed all of the blonde peach fuzz on my legs standing at attention. It was the first time I noticed my hairy legs and I hated it.

Why do none of my friends' legs look like this? I've got to ask them about it today. The thoughts wandered through my mind.

I kept my gaze down at my feet, getting lost in the rhythm of placing one in front of the other, allowing memory to guide my turns until I unexpectedly reached a row of chairs on the sidewalk.

Today was 8th grade graduation.

Facing the school, the rows of chairs began to fill with my classmates. I enjoyed middle school much more than elementary. At least here half of the students were Mexican, and half of the classes were taught in Spanish, so the name-calling stopped after 5th grade.

I no longer stood out; instead I became more invisible. And today would confirm the transparency of my existence to my family.

Parents, grandparents, and other family members began to fill the front lawn of Hill Middle School, their heads bobbing and weaving through the crowd to get a glimpse of their loved one snapping pictures.

I wondered how invisible I was…

Would I even show up in the background of these images?

It was my turn to walk across the stage, to leave another portion of my childhood behind and grow into my future.

"Saharah Pa..Pa..Pareeo." My principal did not bother saying any part of my name correctly before he gestured me to come his way.

My gaze moved from him to my feet as I shuffled across the stage. Not looking up at him, I placed my fingers gingerly around the vanilla colored certificate and exited.

I walked myself down the long hallway to the cafeteria where there was a huge square yellow cake with white frosting. Waiting in line I began to scan the room. Maybe I just didn't see my mom or uncle come in. Maybe they couldn't spot me in the crowd because I was shorter than so many people. Just maybe…

With cake in hand, I scanned the cafeteria one more time with no luck. The second set of doors led to a courtyard where more families were sharing the sweetness of cake, love, and the accomplishments of their 8th grader.

Standing atop the stairs, I had the bird's-eye view of all these clusters of love.

My loneliness pinched my skin like thousands of rose thorns. I became so uncomfortable, the heaviness in my chest dropped into my belly. I felt weak. I drifted in and out of my current circumstance. I couldn't stand there alone one more second.

I escaped the confines of my body and floated away, again. Watching myself from outside of my body was a safe place that held my existence when the reality of my life became too much for my emotional vocabulary.

I hovered in the tree limbs of the courtyard and watched myself from a distance for the rest of the morning.

She just stood there as she was pulled and pushed in and out of pictures by friends and their parents. She forced a smile but if you looked closely, you could see her eyes were empty. There was no voice left in there. No spirit.

By the time I was half done with my cake, a mom of a friend noticed I was alone. She put a bend in her knees to look into my vacant eyes and asked, *"Where is your family?"*

I looked down and mumbled, *"I don't know."*

She smiled uneasily and stood up, grabbing the side of my head and pressing it into her soft, warm, nurturing body. She tilted my chin up with her other hand and looked down at me with a tender smile and a look of sadness or pity in her eyes.

It was a sentiment I had never experienced: someone validating my pain. Her expression punctured my heart. All my pain began to seep out. I pulled away slowly with a crooked smile.

I walked away and right out of the front door of the school. I'm not sure she noticed. I don't think anyone did.

ABANDONED VOICE

This portion of my life is where I operate from the most. I abandoned any worth left to my voice or existence.

This is what I meant in chapter 1 when I shared that your process may not take you back to the very beginning.

My experience in Iran with the war and the revolution shushed my voice out of fear.

But the emotional scar that altered my voice the most was the first five years we were in the States.

The way my voice changed between the ages of 9 and 13 rules over my automatic reaction to life.

The two moments I just shared with you are the experiences that repeated the most for me in my mind and controlled my voice for the next 12 years. Later in this chapter, I'm going to ask you to think about what memories or events come up a lot for you.

I had finalized in my heart that I was not important to anyone.

I built a fort around my heart; no one was allowed in, and my voice made sure of that. I never expressed my real emotions, troubles, or even day-to-day activity to anyone. No one knew the real me.

I was proud that I would never let anyone know me enough to hurt me. Besides, who would want to know me?

When I closed my heart, my voice echoed its sentiment and closed my ability to receive anything—love, help, support.

I became so closed that at the age of 17, I moved out and wouldn't allow my mom to help me financially with my living expenses or college. Stubborn, broken voice.

I ultimately made life a lot harder on myself by keeping my shushed and abandoned voice in charge until I was 25.

To this day, it is difficult for me to come home and automatically talk about my day without the other party inquiring. When someone asks, it validates that I have a right to share. Which, clearly, I do anyway.

I have accepted this as a part of my process. I stay conscious of my walls when they reappear. By doing so, they crumble faster and faster.

Your automatic reaction is a reflection of how you see yourself, other people, and the world.

The voice of your automatic reaction has been in there a while and is rarely heard as it speaks in a split second, and she does so without your consent.

I was physically abandoned by my father and emotionally abandoned by my mother. The combination of these two distinct events in my life changed the voice deep within me for a very long time.

A part of me closed, and it became my automatic reaction to only rely on myself.

This is a part of me that to this day, well into my thirties, I deal with. By being closed, I was the giver in all of my relationships, never the receiver.

I even had tattooed on my rib: *mi don, mi maldición*—my gift, my curse—for the ability I have to give and give and give a tad more, without receiving.

As a woman, I'm sure you can relate. It is in our nature to give.

But this gift leaves us empty, and this gift is a voice so deeply ingrained I have to free myself of it still, by simply being aware it's there. Acceptance.

Through a conscious practice, which included writing, a ton of walking meditation (2x a day), yoga, and the constant state of permission, I have worked through the layers of my automatic reaction.

Respect your process and look forward to the journey of getting to know yourself better.

Today, I am aware of this automatic reaction. When my blocks resurface, I am aware and choose to surrender to the fear; the wall I built many years ago is just an illusion now. A bad habit. I trust to receive love, from myself and from others in my life.

To understand what your automatic reaction is, I want you to dig a little deeper by putting down this book and meandering through your mind.

This is a safe space. Breathe with me.

Look up from this page, close your eyes, relax the muscles in your face.
Scoot back in your seat, even if you're sitting in bed, and uncross your legs.
Now, sit heavy, feel your glutes relax & your tailbone melt down, breathe in deeply.

Reflect on events that seem to come up a lot for you, visually or verbally.
These are events that have left a strong emotional impact on you, the negative kind.
They can be something you experienced long ago or just last month.

Okay, take a little time to sit or lay down with these thoughts.
Other thoughts will come up; just keep detaching from them. "Shush" them aloud if you need.

Put on relaxing music (Pandora's Yoga, Yogini, or Indian Flute stations are my favorite).

If you're feeling restless, go for a walk with <u>full intention</u> to reflect on important moments in your life that are still with you.

Go somewhere that you will not run into people you know. The fewer the distractions, the better. Leave the dog at home so you can get into a good groove. Get lost in the rhythm of your breath and steps.

Take your time.

Give yourself permission to be with these thoughts and the feelings that arise for you.

Write all the events that came up for you. Detox them from your conscience.

Has it been a long time since you've taken some time to reflect like this?

Give yourself credit for going there. It's not the most pleasurable experience. Just because these thoughts are with you a lot, doesn't mean it's fun to revisit the details. That's how you face your pain and eventually walk through it to your voice.

I'm proud of you.

It's time to be your own nurturer. Give yourself permission to be your own healer.

We all need that non-judgmental love that says, you know what…

…yeah, that sucks.

…I'm sorry, baby girl.

…you should not have been treated that way.

…you did make the wrong decision, but that's okay!

I'm going to offer you the space to do this now through a series of questions. You can find more copies of this at www.FindYourVoice.center.

For now, pick just one event...

Describe the situation:

Why do you think you went through this?

Who or what can you point a finger at when it comes to this situation?

Who do you think is responsible for this situation now?

How would you like to have acted/reacted at the time?

What are the thoughts that are left with you because of this event?

What emotions do you have tied with this experience?

What do you think the people involved in this situation were going through?

What do you wish you had said or did?

How do you feel now, writing about it?

How do you think this situation impacted your life and decision-making?

Offer yourself soothing statements when it comes to this. A hug, an apology, an added effort—whatever it is, express it to yourself here:

Give yourself gratitude for taking time to honestly answer these questions. Did you feel a change in your emotions or physical state?

You're building a beautiful practice of checking in with your thoughts, emotions, and body.

Begin to include these connections in your journals.
It's important to feel life below the shoulders.

Let's reflect on your current voice…

What have you noticed in the process of gathering your thoughts in your journal, notes, or in the way you've answered the questions in this chapter? Was this hard? Are you blocked and "just don't know"?

Are you feeling lighter, heavier, or blocked inside?

Do the words or images floating in your conscious have a positive or negative tone?

What thought or theme seems to repeat the most?

Do you find a particular area of judgment towards yourself or others?

What emotions have you been having after these thoughts?

Where are you feeling vulnerable?

How are you wanting to be rescued from this?

What negative behaviors have you been experiencing?

Finding your voice is becoming your own healer.

We have a gut instinct as women; it's our most authentic voice.

Trust that this instinct will reflect on what you discover through these pages and direct you in the most favorable way.

Learn to listen to the voice of reason within yourself.

My voice of reason until I was 25 **blamed** both of my parents.

My constant issues with self-esteem were blamed on my mom to the point that my therapist's only answer was to sever my relationship with her.

When I lay beneath man after man in my teens, not able to say anything, although I screamed *no, no, NO* in my head, I blamed my father.

I blamed because the voice of nurturing had become extinct in my life.

I had no example of a voice that validated how much my young life had gone through.

Rather, most of my family assumed I was too young to remember anything from my life in Iran. And we rarely spoke about my American existence. Even within my own home I felt like a second-rate citizen as my brother went to private school and I to public.

It wasn't until I was able to be my own nurturer, to give myself the space to blame my parents with no guilt or anger, that I was able to soothe those pains, fine-tune my voice.

Now, this took years to do. So, again, respect your process.

I had to be my own teacher, so I hope that bringing this into your conscious in a structured way will make your healing process more efficient.

The series of questions you just answered is **your blame game.**
The event(s) in your life that serves as a block for you.

It's time for you to be the shero of your story.

You are going to rescue yourself. It is time to stop being the victim.

Now, waves of sadness, *it's just not fair,* frustration, and other emotions unique to your story will come. It sucks that the cards you were dealt left this negative impression on you. But now it is your **responsibility.**

When I asked you a few pages back who is responsible for this event now, **what did you write?**

If you said, "Me," you answered correctly.

You are the one left with the pain.
Your voice is the one that is altered by this event.
And it is your most authentic voice that will rescue you.

Let's get closer to that voice first.
To close this chapter, I'm going to offer you tools to get closer to your **automatic voice.**

Don't worry about knowing the difference between your automatic voice and the one inside of you ready to come out—your authentic voice.

Your job is to listen and record.

When you feel a shift in your emotions for the worst, after a stream of thoughts that led you to a particular emotion, decision, or action, **pay attention.**

What part of the situation is repeating?

Are you feeling tired, drained, and unmotivated?

Did you get a heaviness in your chest or tummy?

Are you analyzing a decision over and over?

What are your feelings now about your decision, after some time has passed?

Are you repeatedly telling yourself the outcome, even though you have no control over it?

Just as your skin serves as a sensory pad to protect your body from sharp or hot objects, your inner voice will make you feel uneasy when you make decisions that are not in line with her true craving.

Now, when you are challenging yourself in a positive way (setting boundaries with family members or asking for a raise), you will also feel sensations, like anxiety (excitement dressed up) that has you going over and over the details.

She will be filling in the blanks and answering what the other party thought of you.

Listen and record.

Tune into your thoughts as you have been, and let's add to your awareness the emotions and actions that follow your voice.

I mentioned that my automatic voice was built from two rather significant issues—low self-esteem and the inability to speak up with men.

The layers and process I'm talking about is something to stay aware of. Otherwise you will have expectations that are unrealistic.

Don't tear apart your brain and emotions searching for the overlying issue, unless you already know what it is.

You are a phenomenal woman. Respect your pace. Respect all the voices within you.

Small, daily events like being stuck in traffic or not getting a phone call returned also stir up your automatic voice.

EVENT	FEELING	AUTOMATIC VOICE
Stuck in traffic for 2 hours	Frustrated Irritated Stressed Annoyed	Why me? It's not fair It's awful Can't stand it

I encourage you to take at least 48 hours to yourself. Maybe visit chapters 1 and 2, but don't move forward. Instead, get to know yourself like a new friend, delightfully curious with no judgment.

Continue to record your voice and become aware of how it alters your emotions and behaviors. You don't have to make a lot of time in your day, just bring your awareness with you.

We are in a state of no judgment or attachment.

Do not put the pressure of perfectionism on yourself.

Right now is about turning inward, not about being fixed.

To build the practice of becoming unattached to your thoughts, I've made a gentle yoga sequence with guided meditation for you at www.FindYourVoice.center. It's under "Free Resources" and titled as a chapter 2 resource, *Abandoned Voice*.

Now is a great time to allow someone you trust to be a safe place to practice your voice.

On the next page you will find fun and casual activities to fine-tune that beautiful voice!

What I mean by fine-tuning is being who you are and allowing yourself more snippets of time to be conscious of what you're saying and feeling, in the moment.

You may feel awkward, like you're taking some huge timeout in front of everyone. The reality is, you can check in with your inner voice in just 3–5 seconds.

FINE TUNE YOUR VOICE

Closet Detox

There's nothing like a good girlfriend. Sometimes that can be your mom, aunt, or cousin. Invite her over, prepare something nice to drink, and head to the closet for a detox!

We ladies have two things in common: we all put clothes on (our armor), and we all use words. So the closet is a beautiful space to learn about yourself.

Don't feel obligated to tackle the whole closet. Maybe just pick one section—like party dresses, pants, skirts, shoes, or tees. Go through and decide what to give away.

If you have a memory attached to a particular piece of clothing, talk about it. Notice your tone when you speak of it and how your automatic voice comes into play inside.

Are you embarrassed or amused by your old style?
Are you telling yourself you need to be skinnier or have better boobs or a cuter butt?

If a closet detox doesn't sound like your thing, no worries.

There are always nooks and crannies in the house with sentimental value that can use some sprucing up. How about all those digital photos you've been wanting to organize, delete, and print?

Catch Up Coffee

Invite someone you haven't seen in a while to catch up. This needs to be someone who is neutral or positive in your life.

Be your own nurturer by offering yourself safe situations in which to practice your voice.

The goal here is the same. Try your positive voice, and tune in to your automatic voice within.

When your friend asks you what's new or what you've been up to, you don't necessarily have to mention this book, but do mention positives you are working on.

This is not for you to get your friend's feedback or validation of your life, but for you to practice speaking and listening to both your inner and spoken voice.

HEAR. HERE.

Here is a little bonus resource for you to help tune in to your inner voice. When your automatic voice is making you feel bad, ask her for some evidence about what she is thinking. This space of judgment shows what your automatic voice thinks you deserve, or what you are capable of.

My inner voice says...
It's not fair she got a raise before I did. I'm never going to make more money.
Why didn't she/he call me back? I bet she/he is pissed off.

The evidence not supporting my thought...	The evidence supporting my thought...
It's not fair. I do have more seniority and do a good job.	I have never even approached my boss about a raise, maybe I could get one too.
Yes, it's taking them longer than usual to call back, which makes me feel anxious.	I haven't done anything to upset her. If I did, it wasn't intentional, and I can talk to her about it. She is probably just busy.

Three

THE NURTURING VOICE

SURVIVAL MODE

WINTER 1995 ~ AURORA, COLORADO ~
OVERLAND HIGH SCHOOL

I admired my clean Pontiac LeMans as I walked towards it. I got her a few months after my 16th birthday. She was my safe haven. She made it much easier to escape my life at home, the one I'd been running from since I started high school.

Sliding my left arm out of my backpack, I swooped it to the right to get my car keys. I heard footsteps running up behind me from the direction of the cafeteria.

"SAHAR, *wait, hold up…*"

I knew who it was before I turned around—the first guy who'd befriended me when I transferred to Overland High School.

The first person I'd had casual sex with, and the guy who would tarnish my reputation at this school forever.

Ty stepped in front of me with a genuine look of remorse on his face. *"I'm sorry. For real, I'm really sorry about what's going down."*

In an effort to keep any self-worth I had left, I didn't let myself look at the ground. I couldn't look at him either. I looked past him, past the parking lot, and into the noiselessness.

I was silent. As I often was when I lay beneath Ty, and many of his friends.

It had been a proud moment for him. An experience he shared with his friends—not just the way he was able to be intimate with me, but also *how* he was able to get there. What he did with me. How he taught me.

It's a pretty easy setup when you're dealing with an abandoned girl who was introduced to sexual activity around 6 years old.

Just a little bit of attention, the right words, and my inability to speak up always left me naked on my back.

Sometimes tears would fall into my ears before I noticed how long I had zoned out.

I didn't bother flying out of my body anymore to watch it from above. I would just disconnect, stare past the body on top of me, through the ceiling, and into the silence.

I didn't drink or do drugs in high school, but I became addicted to the attention of the opposite sex. A silent habit I didn't even recognize in my shame coma. One that was spoken about loudly in the hallways of this high school, thanks to Ty and my silenced tongue.

None of the girls wanted to be my friend from the beginning; now that I was the easy conquest among the boys, they hated me even more.

Ty got down on one knee.

The right corner of my mouth raised slightly, an amused quarter smile as I thought, *This is what it looks like when a guy proposes.*

Instead, there he was, kneeling before me in front of the windows of the cafeteria, apologizing that the school thinks I'm a hoe.

I couldn't accept his apology because it was true. I hated what I did and who I was.

I just wanted to go back to George Washington High School, where there was a certain innocence about getting in trouble for just being out late. Mom had even followed me one night and saw I wasn't doing anything bad, just hanging out.

Still, she'd insisted I transfer to another school. My grades excelled, as did my loneliness and my ability to lie to my mom.

As I excelled in class work, I became, on paper, the girl mom wanted me to be. I was in all kinds of after-school activities, enriching myself, growing my brain... as far as she knew. She offered me more freedom and questioned me less about what I was doing.

I tried to push down the weight of my pain by letting someone heavy lie atop me.

I looked down at Ty and said with no emotion, "It's cool."

"But you're still gonna leave?" he asked as he raised his thick football stature back to a standing position.

I nodded yes as I stepped to his right and walked to my car.

I can't believe my scheme to go back to GW worked, I thought, happy, relieved, and filled with joy about going back to my friends—and my innocence—at my first high school.

Two weeks earlier, when the sexual bullying became too much, I had found the courage to speak up. I'd headed straight for the administrative office and asked, *"How can my mom withdraw me from the school if she is unable to show up in person?"*

I had not premeditated this idea. I was in survival mode.

I knew I couldn't speak up with the boys. But, I had practiced the voice of being a perfect, polite girl for a very long time. The voice of an acceptable girl that was rarely up to no good. The kind you trust at face value.

"All your mother needs to do is submit a letter with your name, her signature, a statement that you are withdrawing from Overland, and where you will be attending," the secretary informed me.

"Perfect, have a good day!"

I had not been this excited since Gabriel asked me out on our first date my sophomore year at GW. Now there was a chance to reunite for my last semester as a high school student.

For a week after that, I would retreat quietly to my room after dinner to practice my mom's handwriting and signature, until the perfect transfer letter was scripted.

My stomach in knots, I drove to school and imagined how I would turn the letter in. I started imagining a big conversation with the counselor about how my caring mom wanted to send me back to GW to graduate with my friends.

A wave of sadness came over me. I glided right through a red light. I didn't even look back. I felt my body get heavy, and my cheeks melt down on my face. There was nothing true about that scenario.

The relationship my mom had with me wasn't with the real me. She knew the very small parts of me I trusted her to know. Even those parts were illusions I would paint for her—the daughter I thought she wanted. She would never agree to transferring the real me back, but I had to rescue myself from another experience of sexual silence.

I didn't think much more about what I would say, just followed the burn in my stomach as I walked to my counselor's office.

My moist palms held an envelope that could lead me to freedom or a lock up. I put it on her desk and noticed its wavy texture because of my moist hands.

"Here is the letter from my mom requesting to transfer me at the end of this semester."

"Okay, sounds good. I will process it," she looked up at me over her computer screen, her hands still on the keyboard.

"Thank you," I said casually. I walked out and straight to the bathroom where I sat on the toilet and emptied my upset stomach through first period.

***

The bell rang twice, and a huge smile spread over my face, despite the warning that I only had one minute left until class.

The bell had a certain tone to it that made me happy, or maybe I was just so happy to be back in the groove at George Washington that I didn't care I was going to be late. It would be my first for this semester, and we were already 4 weeks in.

I parted the greasy red paper and took a pinch of the warm chocolate chip cookies that were sold three-for-a-dollar at the student store. I thought it was such a steal.

I let the first bite cuddle with my tongue before rushing to class. The warm dough and chocolate melted, a warm sweetness that made me feel at home.

Separating the greasy paper to get another bite before class, I turned the corner blindly. As the sweetness met my tongue again, I saw Gabriel walking towards me.

He had a neatly folded note that he slipped between the greasy red paper and the binder I was holding.

"I like having you back in these hallways." His deep voice vibrated my heart. He walked away and gave me a smile that let me know just what he was thinking.

THE NURTURING VOICE

I got through most of my last semester in high school without anyone knowing I had transferred. I actually got a steady boyfriend and had an abortion before my mom realized I had switched schools.

A week before prom she spotted my car in the parking lot, and soon after discovered I had transferred. The school discussed pressing charges, and for a while we weren't sure I would graduate because of it. But I did graduate, at the age of 17, and survived the most awkward ceremony.

I thought my mom would be livid when she found out I transferred. Although she was mad, she stayed relatively calm and tried to understand me more. Just like when she found out after the fact that I had an abortion, when I begged for her help because of the pain.

There was an odd sense of pride in her tone as we talked about my choices, because I'd made the decision to nurture myself. Once she found out more, she agreed I had made the best decisions for my well-being.

She recognized my efforts and emotional savvy and asked me to take my focus, energy, and courage, and point it in a more positive direction. The dean agreed.

What they didn't understand was that my negative emotions gave me the courage to rescue myself. It took me a decade after that to forgive myself for the boys I'd slept with. If I had added any more to the roster, that process would have taken even longer, and perhaps had worse outcomes than an emotional scar.

You cannot rid yourself of negative emotions.

That is not finding your voice.

Instead, you have a beautiful chance to realize that not all your negative emotions are bad. You can feel nervous, sad, irritated, embarrassed, or even disgusted in a healthy voice.

Knowing, hearing, and feeling your emotions is healthy.

When you feel capable of handling the emotions by hearing them out, sitting with the feeling, and offering it a healthy voice to express itself, this is finding your voice.

When your emotions begin to feel overwhelming, when you've adopted the voice of hopelessness, you are experiencing the unhealthy voice.

The beautiful thing about finding your voice is that it offers you a space to make a choice with your emotions.

Making a choice to give them a healthy voice will keep your emotions from turning into negative actions (overeating, oversleeping, working or drinking too much, excessive retail therapy).

Since beginning this process, you have listened more to your thoughts and have begun to link them to the voice of your various emotions.

Now, I want you to reflect on the **tone of your voice when you are emotional.**

Determine what you are feeling so you can decide if your emotional voice is working for or against you.

You may find that you are experiencing several emotions at the same time. Instead of being overwhelmed by this, **rate the emotions** you are having.

Are you feeling 70% anxious, 20% sad, and 10% frustrated?

Perhaps 50% sad, 50% embarrassed?

The ratio does not matter; go with what feels right to you. Just label and weigh your emotions.

Identifying the different emotions also gives you time to **separate your thoughts from your emotions.**

Your thoughts will go on and on about how bad things are, causing your emotions to intensify.

Switch your perspective by choosing to weigh your emotions, rather than letting your unhealthy voice keep you as a victim.

Let's practice identifying the difference between your thoughts and your emotions.

HEAR. HERE.

The situation:

My mind has been thinking these thoughts about the experience:

When I think these thoughts, I end up feeling these emotions:

_____ %

_____ %

_____ %

_____ %

Do you hear and feel the difference between your thoughts and your emotions?

I remember when a new boy would approach me at Overland. Internally, I was begging myself to say no from the beginning because I knew that once I went out with him, I couldn't say it. My inner voice would repeat:

Say no. Say no. Say no.
Don't go out with him.
Don't start with another guy.
You're going to sleep with another guy. Say no.
Why can't you say no??? Why did you do that? Why are you like this? Slut!!

These thoughts led me to feel shame and disappointment in myself. As I was processing these experiences and forgiving myself, I would feel a mix of sadness, anxiety, and anger.

Let's peel back another layer and get closer to your emotions' healthy and unhealthy voices.

Think, write, and detach. Don't judge your answers. Just let them flow out of you. This is not a space for solutions, but for reveal.

If you're not experiencing a flow, go back and read what you've recorded since starting to find your voice.

What emotions are you sensing (frustration, anger, nervousness, guilt, sadness, etc.)?

Are they healthy (an emotion you can sit with or that motivates you) or unhealthy (an emotion that feels overpowering and drains you)?

Quiet your mind.

Breathe deep into your belly. Feel your lower back expand. Relax the muscles in your face. Embrace your mixed emotions and enjoy the process.

The voice of Nervousness & Anxiety. She loves to speak up when she is not in control and feels vulnerable. The healthy voice of nervousness will actually motivate you to get something done.

The voice of nervousness can show up as worry, concern, apprehension, fear, agitation, tension, edginess, panic, or uncertainty.

I was nervous about what kind of diseases I would catch if I continued as I was at Overland. This voice echoed in my ear until I found the courage to speak up. I put thought into action by always having condoms with me. I almost had a heart attack at the register, but my nervousness gave me courage.

Anxiety is the unhealthy voice of nervousness. Your perspective is telling you that you cannot cope with a threat (losing a lover or a job) when anxiety arises.

This unhealthy voice will translate physically as rapid heartbeat, sweating, shaking, and stomachaches, among many more symptoms.

It's all about flipping your perspective when your nervousness turns to anxiety.

You are much more capable than you give yourself credit for.

Remember how we ended chapter 2? Go back to finding evidence that works for and against your thoughts when you feel your nervousness transforming into anxiety.

Get to know your voice a little better here:

The voice I adopt when feeling nervous is…

The voice I adopt when feeling anxious is…

I especially feel the unhealthy voice of anxiety when...

This emotion usually makes me act...

A time I experienced healthy nervousness was...

The choice I have when unhealthy anxiety speaks up is...

The voice of Frustration & Anger. She usually shows up when she senses that something is unfair or something must be changed.

The healthy side of frustration lets you know something is wrong and needs to be resolved. The voice of frustration will not let you ignore the issue and it motivates you to take the leap.

The voice of frustration frequently shows up as annoyed, irritated, bad-tempered, fuming, furious, testy, touchy, cross, outraged, or mad.

If you do nothing with your frustration, it will fester into a hostile anger, and this is frustration's unhealthy voice.

When you get angry, you don't believe that you can handle the obstacle of your frustration.

The voice of rage strongly affects your body. You grind your teeth, clench your fists, sweat, and have muscle tension.

Sometimes it takes you getting fed-up with something to motivate a true change. But that takes a lot longer if your voice of frustration turns to rage.

The voice I adopt when feeling frustrated is…

The voice I adopt when feeling anger or rage is...

I especially feel the unhealthy voice of anger when...

This emotion usually makes me act...

A time I experienced healthy frustration was...

The choice I have when unhealthy anger or rage speak up is...

The voice of Sadness & Depression. Sadness is a passive gal and speaks up when you're feeling a loss of some sort. She knows this is temporary and you <u>will</u> feel better.

Sometimes the voice of sadness describes herself as disappointed, hurt, blue, distraught, heartbroken, melancholy, sorrowful, dejected, discouraged, mopey, or in a funk.

When the healthy voice of sadness is ignored, she stops trying to improve the situation and becomes hopeless.

She begins to speak as depression, and the body responds with fatigue, crying, headache, stomachache, and change in appetite.

For some of us ladies, like myself, depression is a medical condition that is lifelong. Prescribed drugs and licensed therapists are a great starting point when you are overwhelmed and cannot pull yourself out. They were a big part of my process throughout my 20's.

For me, it was not a cycle I wanted to continue. I trusted that my inner-voice was strong and wise enough to get me through. Although depression runs in my family, I had a choice of how **I** dealt with it.

I chose to not numb it with medicine, but to deal with it cognitively.

The voice I adopt when feeling sad is…

The voice I adopt when feeling depressed is...

I especially feel the unhealthy voice of depression when...

This emotion usually makes me act...

A time I experienced healthy sadness was...

The voice of Embarrassment & Guilt/Shame. She loves to let you know when you have not met her expectations. She makes you feel responsible for what went wrong. She assumes other people are judging you and your actions.

The voice of embarrassment expresses herself as self-conscious, uncomfortable, condemned, at fault, inexcusable, unforgivable, remorseful, mortified, self-loathing, discredited, disgraced, or dishonored.

The healthy embarrassed voice will get you to blush, feel uncomfortable in social situations, keep you from sleeping at night or looking someone in the eye.

When the voice of embarrassment is not heard, she turns to guilt and shame. This unhealthy voice condemns you for not having control over the situation. The voice of shame will isolate you and remind you that others will have no empathy for you.

The voice of shame is what kept me in the cycle of sleeping with men who were below my worth, even beyond my teen years. It kept me silent.

The voice I adopt when feeling embarrassed is…

The voice I adopt when feeling guilty or ashamed is...

I especially feel the unhealthy voice of guilt when...

This emotion usually makes me act...

A time I experienced healthy embarrassment was…

The choice I have when unhealthy guilt speaks up is...

The voice of Disgust & Hatred. She is a strong and forceful voice that comes up as a result of something she finds offensive.

She expresses herself as a feeling of contempt, revulsion, aversion, or distaste to something or someone.

Disgust is a voice that motivates boundaries. But if she is not heard, she will turn to hatred, and her voice will tarnish your ego and have you set boundaries in a tacky way. She will tell you that you are superior to others and that others are unworthy of your consideration.

Your inability to set boundaries when disgusted often leads you to distance yourself from others in an egotistical way. Hatred is one of the most draining emotions, and it will eventually leave you empty and alone.

Don't join the crowd of haters. Find a graceful way to exit this negative energy.

The voice I adopt when feeling disgusted is…

The voice I adopt when feeling hatred is...

I especially feel the unhealthy voice of hatred when...

This emotion usually makes me act…

The choice I have when unhealthy hatred speaks up is...

The voice of Stress & Feeling Overwhelmed. She only speaks up when she is agitated. An external event usually causes her to start thinking about what life demands of her.

She expresses herself as spread-too-thin, strained, tense, or unfocused.

The voice of stress shows up in your body as rapid heartbeat, increased adrenalin, nausea, or dizziness.

When she is not heard, she gets overwhelmed and exhausts herself. She is unable to problem-solve and gets stuck.

The voice I adopt when feeling stress is…

The voice I adopt when feeling overwhelmed is…

I especially feel the unhealthy voice of overwhelm when…

This emotion usually makes me act…

The choice I have when unhealthy overwhelm speaks up is…

The voice of Envy & Jealousy. She believes you deserve better. She motivates you to get something similar for yourself.

She expresses herself as resentment, rivalry, lust, or the green-eyed monster.

When the voice of envy is not heard, she turns to jealousy: an unhealthy tone of fear that someone else will take what is yours. You fear losing.

The voice of jealousy will compare you and leave you unhappy. Your jaw will tighten and the pit of your stomach will hurt because of her.

The voice I adopt when feeling envy is…

The voice I adopt when feeling jealousy is...

I especially feel the unhealthy voice of jealousy when...

This emotion usually makes me act...

The choice I have with unhealthy jealousy is...

Recognizing when your emotional voice turns unhealthy is a **huge step** in finding your voice.

You cannot make these emotions disappear.
Recognize their voices. Offer yourself a choice to not freak out.
Stay calm, even if you're a bit uncomfortable.
Surrender to the uneasy emotion & take responsibility for it.

You are never in control of your outer world.

Things have happened and will happen to challenge your voice and emotional state.
You have to take responsibility by choosing how your process.
Consciously make the choice to have healthy emotions.
You have found **your** voice.

Taking responsibility when it came to my relationship with my mother was the hardest and longest process.

She was absent when we first moved to the States, and I blamed her for it until I was 25.

Until I took responsibility for harboring and treasuring the voice of this pain, it held me stuck.

Once I recognized I had a choice to surrender to the cards I was dealt, I cracked the first layer of freeing myself from this painful, degrading voice.

I was also able to see my mother for the amazing, resilient woman she is. Acceptance.

Her role was survival, and that is why I lost her. Her culture put an emphasis on the man, and that is why her guilt ran deeper for my brother not having a father than it did for me.

I chose to break this cycle when I found my voice. When I took responsibility for what I would do with my story. When I became my own shero.

So, flex those beautiful heart and soul muscles.

Be the shero of your story by rescuing yourself from unhealthy emotions.

Continue to keep your journal and track the relationship between thoughts and the voice of your emotions.

Don't judge yourself if your habit is to take the unhealthy route.

Don't add guilt. Detach from your thoughts, and do your best to listen.

The following pages are more resources for you to get to know your emotional voices. You can also find more copies in the Find Your Voice workbook.

Don't forget to get out of that beautiful head. Visit me at www.FindYourVoice.center for a yoga and meditation practice. Treat yo' self.

In the last 30 days I have felt...

ashamed	guilty	angry	anxious	depressed
irritated	frightened	excited	embarrassed	sad
frustrated	panicky	mad	proud	insecure
disappointed	cheerful	hurt	disgusted	nervous
peaceful	joy	safe	hopeless	helpless
afraid	scared	happy	loving	calm

Write emotions you've been experiencing...

Let's find some emotional themes in your life. Identify and rate the five emotions (sadness, anger, hurt, irritation…) you seem to encounter the most. Rate them on a scale of 1 (weak)–10 (strongest).

RATING 1–10	WHAT I FEEL...

What negative emotions show up the most for you?

If you are still having a hard time labeling and weighing your emotions through normal journaling and these practices, monitor yourself for at least 7 days with this chart or one similar.

OTHER...	HAPPY	SAD	FEARFUL	ANGRY	SITUATION negative or positive	DAY
10% exhausted —going through why my alarm didn't go off and blaming myself made me so tired I couldn't even focus at work.			70% I got pretty anxious about getting written up and maybe even getting fired.	20%, at first I was pissed that my phone alarm didn't work	My alarm didn't go off, and I was late to work.	MONDAY

	65% soooo excited to find an outfit and finally have dinner with my crush!		30% pretty nervous about what to wear, what to say. I hope my palms don't get all sweaty!	5% frustrated that it took him so long!	Brian asked me out on a date!!!	TUESDAY

OTHER...	HAPPY	SAD	FEARFUL	ANGRY	SITUATION negative or positive	DAY
						MONDAY
						TUESDAY
						WEDNESDAY
						THURSDAY
						FRIDAY
						SATURDAY
						SUNDAY

HEAR. HERE.

Vehicle for release

Write the words that are serving as your blocks.

Observe

How have your emotions changed due to these thoughts?

I

How will you give yourself permission to be released from this perspective?

Challenge

Challenge your negative voice here.

Embrace

How can you embrace this part of your process?

FOUR

THE DESTRUCTIVE VOICE

LINGERING ON THE EDGE

WINTER 2005 ~ CHERRY HILLS, COLORADO ~ UNCLE'S HOUSE

I found my red suitcase packed and waiting for me at the front door. I clenched my jaw and thought, *couldn't they at least let me pack my own shit?*

That's the reality: family passes you around when they don't want to deal with your suicidal tendencies.

After my first attempt, my uncle had come to get me from New York. He brought me back to his house in Denver.

The elegant decor and quiet environment of his large house, which I had always admired, weren't as soothing as I imagined. They just reminded me of the distance between me and the life and love I dearly wanted.

My room there had its own bathroom that led out to the pool.

The only thing I liked about Colorado was how sunny it always was, even in the dead of winter. I opened the door that led outside and let the sun fill up the bathroom. Dropping my pillow by the door I turned around to the sink, looked at the reflection of my tired, pale face in the mirror and mumbled: *I'm going to die now.*

I had saved my sleeping pills, mood stabilizers, and antidepressants for this.

I filled my left palm with as many white capsules as I could before tilting my head back and dropping them in my mouth. I kept my head back as I took three huge chugs of water.

The pills went down, but my body began to gag. She knew this was no good. I quickly grabbed a piece of gum, allowing the spearmint saliva to soothe my throat and tummy. With great force I held back my gag by breathing in through my nose and out of my mouth. The pressure on my pulsing stomach made my eyes water.

There was no way I was going to throw up my best suicide plan.

I quickly filled my hand up two more times and swallowed the remainder of my pills. Stepping over my pillow, I pushed it all the way up to the sink cabinets before laying myself down in the sun.

I grabbed my iPod and put The Cure's *Wish* album on repeat and placed both ear buds in. I lay flat on my back and let the sun warm my face as my body melted into the cold tile floor. An image of Ty breaking my Cure cassette tape in half filled the back of my eyelids.

I was 17 when he found it in my room one afternoon when Mom wasn't home, *"Why do you have this depressing music?"*

I shrugged my left shoulder.

"You don't need this shit." Without my permission he had broken my cassette in half.

Eight years later and I felt like my life was singing the same song of sadness and hopelessness. My uncle had taken me in, and his wife had kicked me out.

I don't blame her. I haven't been that great to have around since I turned 25 a few months ago.

My uncle noted my sad face when I saw my suitcase pre-packed and reassured me that going to live with my Mom would be good for my healing process. For our relationship.

I hadn't talked to or seen mom since my first attempt. To ease the awkwardness of our reunion my uncle and his wife said we could stay at their house. My mom wouldn't leave my side.

I had not welcomed a touch from my mom for years. She insisted on spooning me my first night home. My skin resisted her touch. I felt restless, twitchy. I tried not to move, not wanting to wake her, disregarding how angry and frustrated I was. During my teen years, I'd hated that she was such a light sleeper. It made it impossible to sneak out or invite anybody in.

Her small arm felt heavy atop my body. She snored lightly. I could tell she was exhausted.

While I was in a Boulder mental health facility, the unarticulated pain began to find its way out. It made me uncomfortable, but I couldn't run from it. I was again confined to a locked floor. I paced the hallways incessantly.

Unable to run, avoid, or shove down my emerging thoughts, I found no way of getting rid of them other than writing them down. All of them. Anytime they came up. On anything I could find.

I reflected on who I was and the decisions I made because of my intertwoven experiences. I couldn't just point the finger at one thing; there were plenty of options—too many.

Night after night, my mind danced in circles, trying to untangle the hurt and mistakes and assign a blame to each one.

The revolution brought us shame.
The war pushed us out of our home.
The States took away my father and, in so many ways, my mother.

They tried to keep her away from me in the hospital, seeing my fragile state and blaming it all on Mom. I couldn't even wrap my head around all the pain. I didn't want to wake up to face it, or her.

I had been consoling myself by planning another attempt.

I'd had my eye on this extension cord all day. I knew exactly which tree I could climb for what would be my final attempt.

No more of my boyfriend Darrian physically stopping me from hurting myself.

No more of my friend Victor calling randomly after I swallowed a bunch of pills. A phone call I don't remember answering. The phone call that saved my life.

I was finally going to find peace.

Millimeter by millimeter, I shifted my body from underneath her arm. I went back to my tiptoeing teenage years and moved slowly and lightly through the house. I was aware of every obstacle between me and the extension cord. Gently, I maneuvered my way behind the accent table and chair. I exhaled a huge, slow sigh of relief once I had it safely in my hands.

It was cold outside. My pajamas and fleece zip-up did not protect me from the sharp air. It startled me and brought me out of my suicidal trance for a moment.

The moonlight cast a blue hue on the frosted grass. I walked through the frozen yard, hearing the crunch underneath each step. I wished I had socks on. Gloves too.

The splintery, sticky sap from the pine tree did not make it any easier for me. I zig-zagged my way to the only opening between branches that would leave room for my soon-to-be breathless body.

I found two branches heavy enough to hold my weight. One for me to sit on, the other to hang my makeshift noose (which I should have researched better).

My moment of peace was breaths away.

I didn't have to worry about facing my memories. Accepting them. Or letting them go.

My numb fingers moved my long curly hair to the back and slid the extension cord around my neck. I was scared. I didn't want it to hurt or take a long time. This life had been long enough.

I slid my butt all the way off, holding onto a skinny branch with my left hand, pressing my right fingertips against the spine of the tree. I felt the tug on my neck. It made me gag. I stayed for one more gasping breath then pulled myself back up and coughed.

Damn it, Victor!

I was so pissed that my overdose did not work.

This is way harder.............Fuck.

Again, I slid off the branch, much slower, feeling the cord around my neck get tighter and tighter. I gagged again but wouldn't pull myself up— I wouldn't let go either.

I stayed with the uncomfortable decision, watching the clouds made by my warm breath get smaller and smaller.

My hands were hurting from the cold and the splinters. I was so tired of feeling any pain or discomfort. I exhaled my fear, relaxed my face, and let go with both hands.

There was nothing relaxing about the next part.

I choked, my body automatically responded defensively, kicking and jerking, swaying me to hit other branches. I swayed back and forth about seven times before grabbing a branch and pulling myself up again.

Gasping, coughing, crying a river of snot and tears, I held the cord with both hands, surrendering to failure.

My calm place since I was 11 years old was the image of a gun shooting my head. Instead of wanting to find a gun, I wanted to find a way out of this melancholy mess.

I was ready for a new scenario.

I no longer wanted to live this tragic story.

I held the extension cord with both hands when I came back into the house and straight to my uncle's room. I handed it to him and said, "I don't want to be like this anymore."

The next morning Mom took me to the emergency room.

After a few hours of questioning and counsel, I was released under my mom's watch, and with the condition that I would admit myself into the Cognitive Behavior Therapy program at Porter.

That night in the tree would mark my last suicide attempt.

THE DESTRUCTIVE VOICE

Monday through Friday for eight weeks I checked in and out of Porter Hospital for 8-hour days of Cognitive Behavior Therapy (CBT) lectures, group therapy, solo therapy, and the occasional yoga session.

If I didn't show up, the cops would be called.

This was the first hospital that took the therapy approach versus the shove-all-this-medicine-down-your-throat approach.

In New York, they upped my anti-depressants three times in a very short time span, causing my suicidal thoughts to become clearer. To this day, the irony that the one side effect of antidepressants is more persistent and attainable suicidal thoughts makes no sense to me.

What can I say? We live in a society that wants an easy fix.

Shoving your womanly voice down will kill you one way or another.

Respect your process.

It is a process because there is no convenient amount of time for healing a voice that has been hurting for years. You will achieve healing by fine-tuning your voice as she blossoms.

There are layers to healing, and all of them take a different tone within you.

When I was 25, my inner-voice had been shoved down for so long she wasn't having it anymore, and she turned against me out of pure rage.

Before, she was the voice of blame, pointing a finger at the revolution, the war, my dad, and my mom. I put so much energy into blaming that I didn't stop to feel or hear what emotions **I** was experiencing. Instead I tried to cover them up with job titles, shopping, men, drinking, and drugs.

If I had stopped talking blame and started talking emotions, I would not have been filled with such overwhelming hopelessness. My emotions and my process would have been more manageable for me.

At Porter, it was about 20% meds and the rest was about building cognition. Doing a lot of what you have been doing with this book: recognizing cognitive thought patterns. **Especially the destructive ones.**

By the age of 11, I had set up such a protective wall around my emotions that everything in my world when it came to love was black-and-white.

I was born a girl, so dad had no interest, and he left me. I am worthless.
My mom forgot about me and prefers my brother. I am not lovable.
Gabriel abandoned me for my friend. I don't deserve love.

Although my mom tried to reach out to me, I was too used to shutting her out. I had moved out of the house at the age of 17 and kept running.

All the way to my 25th year in New York, where I was able to check everything off my happy list. The job. The money. The man. The view. The wardrobe. The dancing. The drinks.

I had everything I wanted, but my voice was still behind a barrier.
I wasn't feeling anything, just operating on autopilot day-to-day, goal-to-goal.

I had made lists of accomplishments that would make me feel successful or heard.
But in reality, most of those were just geography or credit card debt.

So now it wasn't just love, but every aspect of my life that became **black-and-white.** I was either a failure or a success in all areas of my life.

As a woman, I was in desperate need of some guidance, and all I could hear was the absence of my mom's voice echoing back to my childhood. I became resentful of her after I moved to New York and crossed everything off the "feel-good" list.

I was unable to see that when I needed her the most, she was just a 33-year-old abused woman with no voice, who was abandoned in a new country with no money and two kids.

I could not look deep into the black to see the cycle she was unable to break.
I existed in the blinding white of my voice screaming for attention.
I had ignored the cry of my inner voice too long.

When you ignore the voice of your emotions, she does not shut up.

She repeats.

So much that you don't even hear her anymore. You just start to see the world as she tells you to, silently.

She has a lot to do with your automatic voice we talked about in chapter 3.
Does your internal voice translate your outer experiences in any of the following ways?

Black-and-White voice. She will make you angry and depressed. She believes in success or failure and nothing in between.

As far as I was concerned at 25, my mom had completely failed me. I totally ignored the fact that without her I would not have had a choice or a voice as a woman. I discounted her and added to the negativity that brought her down as a result.

This voice leaves no room for color; she sees in one tone.

Sensitive voice. She often feels guilty and anxious.
She spends a lot of time taking things personally and blaming herself for mistakes.

Forgetting a lunch date or having a friend cancel plans will repeat in her head and she will find a way to blame herself for it all or take it personally.

Dramatic voice. She will make you angry or depressed.
She thinks in an all-or-nothing kind of way:

This always happens to me!
I'm never going to outgrow this mistake!

She doesn't see the world as a fair place, but one that is continuously sending her challenges. She is pretty bitter about it.

Negative Nancy voice. She loves to stress you out and get you to worry. She will ignore all of the positives and make sure you stay the victim.

She loves to go to the dark nooks and crannies of your every day. She is a very judgmental voice that will talk you out of just about anything.

Psychic Voice. She loves to embarrass you and make you antsy.
She will tell you what other people are thinking and feeling about you.

She will assure you that the person you are interested in does not like you.

When you think you can achieve a big goal, she will remind you of how embarrassed you will be when you fail.

Tragic Voice. Watch out for this one; she loves to take over. She will hold your hand and take you down the path of anxiety, worry, and depression.

She will remind you that all situations end badly and that you can't do anything about it. She will take your voice and make it hopeless and incapable.

As a woman, you have many voices.
You are a person who is capable of the most genuine empathy.
You also have the voice of reason and strategy. You can prepare for the future.
You are quite a capable and magnificent being.

With no judgment, I want you to sit with these descriptions and bring their voices to the pages of your journal.

Here is a suggested format:

BEHAVIOR	EMOTION	VOICE	EVENT	DAY
Thought about what I would buy my friend and how I was going to apologize. I stayed home to rest and ended up not feeling rested because of all the guilt.	sad & guilty	Psychic voice told me that I was going to lose this friend forever and I was a bad friend.	I canceled plans	MONDAY
Totally started to ignore her at work, and some of the people she hangs out with. Isolating myself more.	lonely & anxious	Sensitive voice told me it's probably because she doesn't like me, and I think my e-mail last week sounded offensive.	I didn't get an invite to my co-worker's birthday party	TUESDAY
				WEDNESDAY
				THURSDAY
				FRIDAY

Hopefully you've given yourself some time to take a break to journal or spend a few days getting to know the process of your voice.

As it goes in finding your voice, this is another layer of discovery. Knowing is half the battle, sweetheart.

So, what do you do when you've met the psychic, negative nancy, or drama queen voice within you? Start to question her.

For her voice to lose credibility in your thought and decision-making process, she needs to stand up to the facts.

By the time I had gotten to the CBT program at Porter, I had already done some digging and gotten to the root of my problem. But not speaking and operating from this place was a different task. I had to face my black-and-white voice repeatedly and discredit her with two questions.

1. I asked her for **evidence** that **I was unlovable.**

My voice reminded me of my parent's physical and emotional abandonment. I rebutted with cold, hard facts.

"I am loveable! I had about a dozen friends that showed up by my bedside last week. Even the nurse said she had never seen one person get so many supporters. She told me it was a reflection of who I really am!"

I ask you, what voice is speaking up for you right now that serves as your block?

What evidence proves her voice to be true?

What evidence proves her voice to be false?

2. I asked her to release the **pressure** she puts on me to **control** the situation.

She wanted me to remember that I have no choice and no control. That no matter how perfect I was, Mom and even my first love, Gabriel, abandoned me.

For many years, I tried to prove my inner voice wrong by becoming a perfectionist.

Then, years down the road, when I had a genuine chance at love with Gabriel, she would not let me voice another perspective of our childhood, only the pain—and recognize the growing pains *he* was experiencing as a man without a father. She pushed him away and my heart was broken again.

I ask you, what voice is speaking up for you that wants you to control the outcomes of your life?

What other perspective can you voice about this situation?

What choice CAN you make in this situation?

You'll get used to questioning your automatic voice, and you'll discover your true voice over and over.

Soon you will have done it so much that your authentic voice will find a clear channel and be heard.

She speaks from the space where YOUR soul and personality connect.

The process of getting to that space includes questioning and affirming.
Affirmations have been around longer than you and me both.
But we are going to give your affirmation a new voice.
A factual voice that you believe.

There is no use in setting a generic affirmation (*I am lovable*) that you automatically rebut. You're just offering yourself more opportunities to repeat the voice that is holding you down.

The voice of your affirmation will not reflect a true change in your voice if you don't believe the affirmations emotionally. Does your inner voice sound anything like this:

Affirmation: I am not a failure.

Back-talk: But I'm **not** doing as well as_____. I feel like I'm failing.

Feeling: Sad, hopeless, unmotivated.

There are two things going on here: the affirmation is vague, and the voice of your back-talk is making an unrealistic comparison. This is the space to be factual, not dramatic.

A more realistic affirmation: If I don't do as well as others, I am not a failure, just human.

Back-talk: I won't compare myself. Other people have other paths. Even if I achieve 80% of my goal, I have not completely failed.

Feeling: More confident, motivated, hopeful

Try this simple method when you notice the words in your head talking you back into your negative core belief (block).

Realistic affirmation + Fact-based back talk = Embodying new voice

Your turn...

Realistic affirmation:

Back-talk:

New voice:

Your voice sometimes doesn't speak up in words though.

She often expresses herself in images, day and night dreams, or just flashing images that pop up, based on memory or foreseeing something negative.

Luckily, when you have the power to create these images or bring them up, you have the ability to change them.

Offer yourself space to write or draw these images in this book or the pages of your journal.

Images that cause you stress are usually not based on the reality of the situation. They often voice the worst-case scenario to yourself.

Just like we questioned and wrote an affirmation against the voice that rules your process, I want you to take what you are imagining and walk around the scenario. Literally see it from another perspective:

Focus on another ending. Don't change the event, but take responsibility for the ending.

I could not change the visual of my mom not coming to my 8th-grade graduation. But I took responsibility and changed the ending by having a beautiful relationship with my mom. I *changed* the ending. More than in my mind, my voice brought it to life.

As we end this chapter, I offer you two practices: one to use your true voice and another to quiet them all.

You've been in your head a lot. I want you to practice your true voice by picking a conversation that needs to be had.

Don't make this a big thing; make this a **sharing** thing.

Time to meet up with an old or new friend, a family member, perhaps an acquaintance, or even a stranger—whomever you feel comfortable practicing with.

You can pick someone's brain, or share your process with someone, or catch up with someone you haven't seen in a while just to hear how you speak of yourself lately.

Think of at least three people and make a solid date with them. A person you can talk on the phone with, Skype, FaceTime, or meet in person. You just have to be talking, not writing, emailing, or texting—use your voice.

Practice sharing your opinion.
Practice sharing your strengths.
Practice sharing your struggle.

Practice listening to someone else without feeling down, judgmental, or comparing yourself inwardly.

Remember these conversations are not about confrontations; an informational call about someone in a position or industry you're interested in may be all you need to get you started.

Just think of it in terms of step-by-step. Have talking points or questions prepared, and listen to your voice process—which view you are taking (drama, negative nancy, etc).

Let's break down the conversations you need to have with someone....

Who is a good person(s) to practice this conversation with?

Do you have an inward or outward goal for this conversation?
(Inward: I don't want to discount myself once during the talk. Outward: I want to be brave enough to ask for her mentorship.)

What do you picture talking about?

What are you comfortable sharing?

What voices are coming up for you right now?

Have you been keeping yourself from having this conversation?

I've created a beautiful yoga practice for you about letting go of control. It's found at www.FindYourVoice.center.

If you're not in the mood for yoga, please do something physical. Give yourself permission to spend some time with your body, below the shoulders, guilt free.

Please offer yourself an opportunity to quiet the voices.

BREAK THE CYCLE

Vehicle for release

Write the words that are serving as your blocks.

Observe

How have your emotions changed due to these thoughts?

I

How will you give yourself permission to be released from this perspective?

Challenge

Challenge your negative voice here.

Embrace

How can you embrace this part of your process?

FIVE

THE VOICE OF PERMISSION

BIG CITY OF DREAMS

WINTER 2007 ~ NEW YORK, NEW YORK ~ TIMES SQUARE

*B*efore leaving the gala, I stood in front of my life-size resume that was on display in the ballroom lobby. My eyes scanned the bullet points, noticing the shift from banking to fashion since recovering from my depression.

My whole life had gotten a makeover in the last two years.

I nodded my head in approval of my decision to move back to my New York apartment a few weeks after being released from the program at Porter Hospital in Denver.

A sigh of relief escaped me as I gazed up and beyond my resume to the wall of windows that faced Times Square.

Now, my blood-red Mary Janes and I stood there above the heart of Manhattan, with a check for $5,000. I had just been awarded a scholarship by the Young Men's Association Fashion Education Fund.

I wore my creamy white Kenneth Cole coat because I knew Kenneth and his brother, Neil, would be there.

I had received word a few days before that for my last semester at LIM College, the coveted internship position at Iconix would be mine, and Neil Cole happened to be the CEO.

This was my chance to invest in a career, to be brave enough to be seen, to be unforgettable, to step into the adult life my 29-year-old voice was craving.

I zig-zagged through the ballroom at the Marriott, looking for the Cole brothers and rehearsing my opening line:

"Hi Mr. Cole. My name is Sahar, and I can't wait to start learning from you and your company next semester!

"Hi Mr. Cole! When I heard you would be here I knew I had to introduce myself and share with you my excitement for the opportunity to intern at Iconix!"…that's better, maybe I should say…

All my preparation came to an abrupt stop when a well-dressed, tall, lean, white-haired man appeared a few steps ahead of me. Tim Gunn, the creative lead at Liz Claiborne and the most gracious fashion mentor in the whole industry. I watched him religiously on *Project Runway* and now he was just a few steps from me.

My feet walked forward, my mind blank, and my palms moist. I went straight up to him and said: *"Thank you so much for what you've done for fashion!"*

His eyebrows raised in genuine surprise. "Why, thank you!"

I think I had caught both of us off guard with my enthusiasm and huge smile. I managed to gather some clarity and asked to have a picture with him.

I never did find Mr. Cole that night, and it turns out I didn't need to; my new voice would allow me a 1:1 with Mr. Cole when I secured a position with the company a few months later.

My clutch purse vibrated and a smile grew on my face. I knew it was Robi texting me that he was there. I couldn't bring a guest to this award ceremony, but he had gone with me to all the others. It had become one of my favorite feelings to dress up and share my achievements with someone.

He was my special someone. The someone who knew and saw me in a way that helped me see myself in a new light.

Tiptoeing onto the escalator I buttoned up my luxurious creamy coat and got ready to embrace my love.

"*Sahar Jon!*" He welcomed me warmly with a single rose and open arms.

No one in my lifetime had looked at me the way he did. His gaze was the softest, safest place I had ever existed.

"*How was it, BAEEE-BEEE!?,*" a genuine excitement that, for me, was such a foreign expression of love from a man. An expression that celebrated all of my small moments. An experience I had never had.

"Amazing! Cha-ching! Check this out!" I whipped out the check from my coat pocket and brought it between our faces.

That didn't stop him from smiling and kissing me, crushing the check between our noses. The back of my eyelids sparkled yellow and red from all the lights in Times Square. He leaned into me and I couldn't help but finish the movie-like moment by raising one leg.

A few blocks from here is where this love story started.

It was the silhouette of his shadow in a dark movie theatre that first captured my attention. Turns out it was his documentary I was watching. Four hours later we were locking lips outside of the Hard Rock Cafe on what became an 8-hour date.

He pulled away slowly. A smile reappeared as he took his right hand and brushed the contour of my face. He had the power to make everything stop. Calmly and from the depths of his heart he shared, *"Proud of you baby. Let's go celebrate."*

He took my hand and led me out of the colored chaos. "I know exactly where to take you." And he always did.

THE VOICE OF PERMISSION

*A*fter leaving Porter hospital, I recognized that there was nothing physical in my way. It was my own voice that always stopped me.

My relationship with my mother was on the mend, but I had no interest in staying in Colorado. All of me longed to be back in New York to give the new me a go at it.

Once I got back, I didn't jump right into things. Being released from a mental health program has its strings attached. I had a full schedule of counselor, psychologist, and psychiatrist to check in with, almost daily.

I was at the end of my 25th year and it was the first time I had found myself without a job since I was 13. Until this point, my self-worth and my paycheck had always gone hand-in-hand.

Now that my true voice had some recognition, she wouldn't let me be a slave to the paycheck. Yet she pressured me to find direction, become successful, ignite change.

"*What is your niche?*" everyone, including myself, wanted to know.

I loved fashion. It was my armor and the first place I found confidence naturally. I knew I wanted to use fashion to empower and give back to the community. But I had no idea where to start.

One afternoon, walking from the train to my psychologist's east side apartment, I noticed a red-and-purple flag waving in the wind. The words "business" and "fashion" swayed mid-air, pointing to what is now my alma mater. But THIS was **not** the *a-ha* moment.

I had transcripts from five different colleges at that point, but no degree. I held shame for being "my age" and not having a degree, so my first instinct was not to go back to school. I didn't have money. I knew I was emotionally smart, but I needed some convincing to remember that I was also book-smart.

That same day, it was not me who gave me permission to go give it a shot and go back to school, but my therapist.

Serendipitously, I didn't need to bring up what I saw outside. It was one of the first things she mentioned to me.

That beautiful invisible spiritual support system is always there. Divine intervention.

Your true voice will lead you to these experiences, always.

Now, it wasn't all rainbows and butterflies after that.

The truth is, I was accepted to a private college with a high price tag and a population of students almost a decade younger than me, and a lot more well-off.

Being a small school, it was very evident to me that I was one of maybe three "older students." This reality often brought on the voice of comparison and embarrassment.

The first year I was constantly comparing myself to my classmates and my old voice would often reappear and tell me to disappear by sitting in the back and not engaging with the class.

My wounds from my recent depression were still too fresh though. I wouldn't let myself lose my voice that quickly. I had worked too hard, and my hunger for growth fueled me to just take one day at a time.

I had to repeatedly give myself permission.

I am smart and deserving enough to win this scholarship.

I am lovable, and I can receive love from Robi without feeling like I owe him anything.

I made a mistake by transferring so many times, but I'm not at the end of the line.

I had to give myself permission to be the 27-, 28-, 29- and 30-year-old student raising her hand.

It's okay that I'm smart and the teacher complimented me in front of the class. I don't need to feel guilty about the attention.

I had to respect me and my process or I would go back to the same voice, the same cycle, the same life.

The process of giving myself permission was almost as exhausting as carrying a 21-credit-hour class load. It takes work, but it is a huge catalyst to finding your voice. You are worth the time and energy.

Now, sometimes this process came with nights of crying and journaling. Nights of sitting on my fire escape thinking: *Should I try to kill myself again?* My voice would waiver, I would visualize it, but never went as far as planning it, like before.

It's tough when you first find your voice. It wavers between the old and the new. You're still trying to find credibility in it.

Let's work towards the next part in your process.

You've listened your voice, and you've tuned into her patterns and process.
Take all that you know, and get to know her tone in the different areas of her life.

Nothing you are writing here is set in stone.
Do not feel the pressure that what you desire has to be put into motion immediately.

Offer yourself permission to be honest and to think boldly about what you crave.

There are more copies of this in the Find Your Voice workbook as well.

Lifestyle:

Career, money, home, space, possessions, fashion, travel.

What do you crave for this area of your life?

What does YOUR voice say about this area of your life?

What does the external voice pressure you to do in this area?
I must have money in order for my voice to count.

What does your voice of comparison say about this area of your life?

In this area of your life, what you are grateful for? Why?

What's not working in this area of your life?

How can you give yourself permission to make this part of your life more in alignment with your voice, what you truly crave?
*I need to give myself permission to ask my boss for a review and a raise.
*I need to give myself permission to save up and use the money to travel.

Body & Wellness:

Healing, fitness, food, rest, mental health.

What do you crave for this area of your life?

What does YOUR voice say about this area of your life?

What does the external voice pressure you to do in this area?

What does your voice of comparison say about this area of your life?

In this area of your life, what you are grateful for and why?

What's not working in this area of your life?

How can you give yourself permission to make this part of your life more in alignment with your voice, what you truly crave?

Creativity & Learning:

Artistic & self expression, interests, education, hobbies.

What do you crave for this area of your life?

What does YOUR voice say about this area of your life?

What does the external voice pressure you to do in this area?

What does your voice of comparison say about this area of your life?

In this area of your life, what you are grateful for and why?

What's not working in this area of your life?

How can you give yourself permission to make this part of your life more in alignment with your voice, what you truly crave?

Relationship & Society:

Romance, friends, family, collaborating, community, causes.

What do you crave for this area of your life?

What does YOUR voice say about this area of your life?

What does the external voice pressure you to do in this area?

What does your voice of comparison say about this area of your life?

In this area of your life, what you are grateful for and why?

What's not working in this area of your life?

How can you give yourself permission to make this part of your life more in alignment with your voice, what you truly crave?

Spirituality

Soul, inner self, truth, faith, practice.

What do you crave for this area of your life?

What does YOUR voice say about this area of your life?

What does the external voice pressure you to do in this area?

What does your voice of comparison say about this area of your life?

In this area of your life, what you are grateful for and why?

What's not working in this area of your life?

How can you give yourself permission to make this part of your life more in alignment with your voice, what you truly crave?

The beautiful part about this chapter is exploring your voice in all areas of your life. You are a versatile being with many desires. There is nothing wrong with being multi-passionate.

Do not be overwhelmed by the amount of ideas or the list of to-do's or shortcomings that have come into your conscious voice.

You cannot fix all the areas of your life at once. Give yourself permission to be exactly where you are in your process.

It begins with one thought, which leads to one action. Something small can be very powerful.

Sometimes it's great to take a break from the internal cleanup and reflect on your progress in the environment you live in.

If you want to get more focus in any area of your life, **start by creating the space for it, literally.** By your surroundings being clean, welcoming, and a reflection of your personality, you are offering yourself a nurturing place for change and renewal.

The changes you make (cleaning your car, buying yourself flowers, painting an accent wall, lighting a new candle) will serve as a daily reminder about the inner change you are making.

Here are a few more ideas to bring a new energy into your space...

...your purse and wallet: clean them out; file or toss those receipts.

...buy a new pillow and lamp to create a new reading and journaling nook.

...reorganize those shelves, print pictures from a recent trip, and make room for journals.

...set up an altar with candles, crystals, flowers, lyrics, and notes to bring out YOUR voice.

The more you can see the time and creative energy you have invested in offering yourself this space, the more you are giving yourself permission to nurture your needs.

After creating your space, invite your current voice to enjoy it with you. Make some house rules to make this space the most nurturing to **your voice.**

I have two areas that I have reserved for me: a small altar in my room and my car. I can lie on my bed and see my altar or I can grab a pillow and sit in front of it. It has pictures, words, stones and necklaces that remind me of my voice.

I often find myself analyzing and thinking a lot when I drive, so I made my car a soothing environment, too. I bought a soft steering wheel cover, I made a meditation CD mix, and I keep my car smelling like lavender.

A few of my **house rules** for my nooks (and daily life):

- Do not focus on your old voice, who you used to be.
- Leave all thoughts of comparison outside of this space.
- Give yourself permission to admire yourself in this space.
- Write cards to the people who matter to you most, with love and gratitude.
- Invite journals, goals, music, and friends that nurture the voice you are growing into.

Your turn. Make a list of a few REALISTIC ideas of how you can create a space of permission for yourself, and set a few house rules.

Ideas:

House Rules:

Please remember to live life below the shoulders! We are going to take more solid steps towards what you crave in these areas of your life in the next chapter. It's vital that you take time to get out of your head before then! There is a guided yoga and meditation for this chapter at www.FindYourVoice.center

I give myself permission to detach from my past when I am building my future.

SIX

THE VOICE OF FAILURE

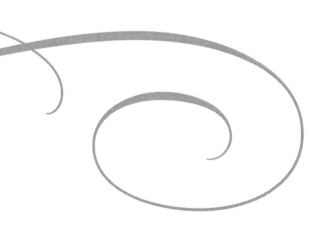

THE NEXT 1,000 DAYS

WINTER 2011 ~ BROOKLYN, NEW YORK ~ MY APARTMENT

My 12' x 12' studio apartment always managed to surprise me with how much space it had.

Never in the three years living there did I feel cramped or regretful that I moved to the ass of Brooklyn to live in a small Victorian space of my own. I understood when I saw the word "quaint" in the Craigslist ad that the space would be small. Once I saw its bay window that faced a well-manicured courtyard with a gazebo, I knew it was the best choice. Graduating college in an economic nightmare didn't leave me with many affordable options.

I lit the dollar store prayer candle and placed it in the window that was open despite the freezing wind chill. I watched the flame flicker, chuckling... remembering the first day I moved in and got bitch-slapped by the 80 degree heat from the radiator. I opened the windows that day and they've stayed that way ever since.

Tilting my head to the side, my eyebrows raised in an *a-ha moment*. I nodded my head in agreement when I drew the parallel between the heat in my Brooklyn apartment and the weather in my new home in Puerto Rico.

I guess I'd been preparing for it all along.

I drew in a huge breath and adjusted my bikini top, a staple in my wardrobe once I made up my mind to leave my beloved island for another.

Every week I took myself on a date night in Union Square. A couple of Lychee martinis and a Chicken Lime noodle bowl at Republic would help me switch from professor to consumer. Forever 21 was always the destination for a cheap treat—a new bikini—that reminded me of where I would be moving to in April.

After a day of hauling empty boxes home, mentoring high school students, or teaching Fashion Show Productions to an array of 20-somethings, I religiously put on my tights, leg warmers, and bikini top for a session of packing, then yoga.

"I can't believe this is my life," escaped from my lips as I turned around to figure out how to make space for my yoga mat among all the boxes.

There were at least 30 boxes piled on every open surface—against the wall, on the dresser, and even on my bed. I used my right foot to move them flush against the wavy mahogany mirror I'd never gotten around to hanging.

"It's been leaning against the wall for more than a 1,000 days," I thought.

Where will I be in 1,000 days?

I had no direction.

The heaviness of this reality brought my body down. I slid against the boxes to the floor, then slithered my way down onto my back.

Stretching my whole body, my hands and arms found space between the stacks of boxes overhead labeled to go to my mom's in Colorado. My feet struggled to find space between the boxes going to my best friend, Amalia, in Florida.

I gave my weight to the warm wood floor and let my eyes wander between the columns neatly stacked, wondering if I was making the right decision in spreading parts of my life across three different states.

I felt so displaced. Belonging nowhere, to no one.

Tears rolled into my right ear, persuading my entire body into a fetal position. I looked under my bed where one more box hid. The box that held the nearly five years with Robi.

"It's really over," I said half aloud before closing my eyes and remembering his gentle voice reminding me that:

"No one will love you like I do."

His love was rare. We both knew it. But how could I stay with someone who emptied me as much as they filled me?

Rolling onto my back, I grabbed behind my knees and rocked myself up to standing.

"NOT GOING THERE!" I sternly said aloud as I unrolled my yoga mat.

I headed straight for the light switch and slapped the lights off in an attempt to black out the reality of how life had failed me, once again.

THE VOICE OF FAILURE

The memory I just shared with you marked the end of the most challenging three years of my adult life.

I clearly remember May 30th, 2008, as a day that filled me with hope. I was graduating among the top in my class, had landed my dream job in fashion, was supported by my family, and loved by a man who knew my talents better than I did.

It all started that August, the day before I was supposed to start a new job at Iconix. I received a phone call from my supervisor who exhaled so deeply upon hearing my voice I already knew that the position was no longer mine. "Dissolved" was the word she used to describe the way the economic crash had devoured my future in fashion.

This was the first time my emotional well-being was truly tested since I'd been released from the hospital in 2005.

My inner voice tried its best to stay realistic, reminding me that the courage and capability I was so sure of before had not changed, only my external environment had.

It was extremely difficult to keep the value of my voice during the next year as I was rejected by the fashion industry and finally hired by a small business with a passive-aggressive owner.

A year and a half into my job as a marketing manager, I realized there is fine line between letting the voice of failure bring you down and using it to fuel your next step.

I'm sure you can relate. Think of a time you have been so fed up that it motivated you, or gave you the courage to make a positive change.

It could have been as simple as saying no, or having the nerve to walk away, or to speak up for someone else.

Reflect on a small or big experience that **you remember with pride.**

Those are powerful moments to draw from and congratulate yourself for.
Take a moment to reflect and make a note of them.
It was early 2009 when I could sense **I was beginning to lose my voice, again.**

I was tired of being paid nothing and spoken down to. My self-esteem was suffering. I needed to find a solution. I went back to my only source of strength, the one thing my voice still felt very strongly about: the idea of using fashion to empower teens.

It took exactly two days to write the curriculum for what turned into three credit-earning programs through my foundation, Free Your Star. After a semester of working full time, fundraising, and running my program for free, I found the courage (because I was too exhausted to feel any fear) to actually charge for the programs.

Each semester, I steadily gained momentum and eventually established partnerships with public high schools. The Free Your Star Foundation awarded its first scholarship recipient in 2011 and continues to do so annually.

The programs were a success, not only for my mentees, but for myself. Developing and launching Free Your Star was 100% a decision made to save my own voice.

My mom and I were getting closer, but I did not trust her enough to be my confidant and mentor. I hoped by giving to and mentoring others I would fulfill that need within myself.

Robi and I had been dating for three years by then. What was the healthiest part of my life began to deteriorate when his voice of fear took over. He confessed to me that he couldn't see us living together or getting married, that all he would do was hold me back.

I stayed in that relationship two more years because of my own wavering voice that refused to accept failure in our relationship. I was scared to take on life by myself.

Turns out, Robi was right. He is a good man for knowing that our different processes were no longer healthy for each other. He needed to process his voice of fear without me.

It wasn't until 2 years later, in 2011, that I did something about losing my voice.

I found the courage to free myself of everything that validated my identity: my relationship with Robi, my well-established programs, my title as a professor, and my life as a fashionable New Yorker.

When I write to you about this now **I beam with pride** about how hard I worked, how many students and women I helped, how fabulously I lived off of so little money, and the fairy-tale love I experienced.

But, during my first year in Puerto Rico, I was exhausted by the feeling that I had completely failed at life in the Big Apple.

This is a strong example of the power your voice has over your true worth and perspective.

And why I remind you to respect your process.

When I finished comparing what I thought my life should look like versus what it was, I realized I had gotten a master's in life while in NY.

The wisdom gained, I now realize, could never equate to failure.

That's the wonderful thing about messing up. It's never a mistake; it's a life experience.

One that leaves you with something unforgettable.

Remember our healthy negative voices? The voice of embarrassment won't let you forget a mistake, and this ensures success for your next go at it.

You can trust yourself for taking responsibility for the issue and know it won't happen again.

Not letting that embarrassment turn to shame and regret is what you have to watch out for.

That ability to recognize and stay in a healthy negative voice **is** finding your voice. Congratulate yourself.

Take a moment to reflect on experiences you voice as failures. Recognize the pearl of wisdom you walked away with because of it.

I failed trying to....

I learned that...

Now I know I won't ever...

The new meaning of this experience is...

I failed trying to....

I learned that...

Now I know I won't ever...

The new meaning of this experience is...

I failed trying to....

I learned that...

Now I know I won't ever...

The new meaning of this experience is...

There are natural ups and downs in life, and yet we paint a picture of perfection to rebut this process.

HEAR. HERE.

Perfection is an illusion.

The fact that you have made it this far into this book lets me know you are a woman of high standards. Ones you intend to continue to meet.

The voice of perfection will pressure you to meet exceedingly high standards, constantly.

She is the voice that demands you do it right or you're a failure.
She will try to control you and remind you that you are not doing it well enough.
She will bring along with her the voice of anxiety, frustration, anger and depression.

Are you recognizing a voice of perfection within yourself? Do any of these sound like you...

You like to do most of the work yourself.

You try to persuade people to think like you.

When you give direction, you offer several details.

You have to organize your space before you start to work.

You prefer or even demand that other people do it your way.

You avoid new experiences if you think you can't do it right.

After an accomplishment, you think of what more you could have done.

You often think about how others are judging all the mistakes you are making.

You feel that you have to do everything well, even the things you are not good at.

The voice of perfection only allows you to see how you have failed.

Can you hear this voice in your life? Let her speak her rules here…

There is nothing wrong with having high standards for yourself.

Often, though, your voice has been shaped by expectations that are not realistic or your own.

As much as my college graduation was a day full of promise, there was a nagging voice within me reminding me that I was *30 and just graduating college.*

I was truly happy, but there are always outside forces (society & family) that confirmed what my voice of perfection was saying…

> …everyone is right, I'm a late bloomer.
> …f***ing loser, you've done this all wrong.

I had to allow flexibility in my way of thinking to take the power away from the voice of perfection that made me feel like I was last in line.

How does your voice of perfection speak to you?
Glance at what you wrote earlier when reflecting on your voice of perfection.

Can you recognize any rigid rules or expectations you've set for yourself?

Do you feel like you have to do something perfect before sharing it with others?

Do you think that you cannot make a mistake or you will look foolish?

Stay aware of this voice, she will make you see things in absolutes.
Everything in her world is black or white. She will convince you that you have failed.

I am not asking you to lessen your expectations from what you want from yourself and in life. Instead, I want you to recognize the feeling of failure or procrastination that the voice of perfection has led you to in the different areas of your life.

I want you to think about how you've "failed" in your perspective.

Recognize any rigid rules you have that equate to success in each area of your life.

I also want you to be honest about your motivators and limitations, your strengths and your weaknesses. Remember this...

By accepting your weaknesses, you are not giving in to them. You are empowering your strengths.

Hold on to this, and let go of perfection. Before you reflect on the different areas of your life, read the example below.

Give yourself some time to look away from these pages and breathe, make some tea, or move to a new seat.

Take your time. Respect your process and the layers that reveal themselves to you once you leave these pages.

How I've failed in this area of my life…
What makes you unhappy about this part of your life?

What I need to feel successful in this area of my life…
The rules, expectations, or control you have put on this area of your life.

The cost of this rule…

Are there any negative consequences for expecting so much for this area of your life?

Motivator: What is your strength in this area?

Limitation: What weakness do you need to accept in this area?

Ritual I can build in this area of my life: what brings you joy about this part of your life? How can you experience it more?

Lifestyle:

How I've failed in this area of my life…

What I need to feel successful in this area of my life…

The cost of this rule…

Motivator:

Limitator:

Ritual I can build in this area of my life:

Body & Wellness:

How I've failed in this area of my life…

What I need to feel successful in this area of my life…

The cost of this rule…

Motivator:

Limitator:

Ritual I can build in this area of my life:

Creativity & Learning:
How I've failed in this area of my life…

What I need to feel successful in this area of my life...

The cost of this rule...

Motivator:

Limitator:

Ritual I can build in this area of my life:

Relationship & Society:

How I've failed in this area of my life…

What I need to feel successful in this area of my life…

The cost of this rule…

Motivator:

Limitator:

Ritual I can build in this area of my life:

Spirituality:

How I've failed in this area of my life…

What I need to feel successful in this area of my life…

The cost of this rule…

Motivator:

Limitator:

Ritual I can build in this area of my life:

This has been a pretty heavy chapter.

You've reflected on what your voice has marked as failure in different areas of your life.

If you've become motivated to make goals and take actions towards improving the quality of a certain area we talked about, choose just one, maybe two, to move forward with.

Spreading yourself thin is a great way to confirm the voice of failure.
You cannot achieve change when you spread yourself thin.

This is not a race. It's a process. It's your one beautiful life.

Your expression and unique voice have something to say that no one else does.
Enjoy your voice today just as much as you will enjoy her in full expression in the near future.

Invite the voice of failure into your journal.

Give yourself room to recognize that what you now see as failure, as wisdom.

Write down her lessons.

When you write about your shortcomings, remember it doesn't mean failure.

Be tender.

Understand that when you recognize what you did wrong, you are not defeated; you have already won the next round.

This is a great time to give yourself permission to try something out of the ordinary: painting, skating, dancing, or cooking. Something low pressure where you can give yourself permission to not be perfect!

As always, there are additional resources waiting for you at www.FindYourVoice.center

BREAK THE CYCLE

My definition of a perfect meal is...

My definition of a perfect day is...

My definition of a perfect present is...

My definition of a perfect body is...

My definition of a perfect love is...

My definition of a perfect me is...

My definition of perfect is...

SEVEN

THE VOICE OF BOUNDARIES

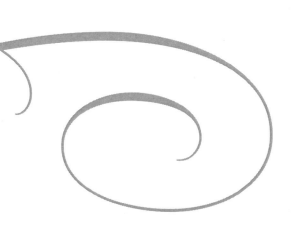

FRESH JUICE

SPRING 2012 ~ OCEAN PARK, PUERTO RICO ~ MY ROOM

*T*he ornate iron door screeched every time a guest returned from their adventures around the island.

The echo of stern footsteps always let me know when it was Sofia, not a guest that had arrived.

I had never befriended a woman with such a strong energy. She was unapologetic about her demeanor, yet extremely aware of how it impacted others. She was a blend of a woman I had only seen on the big screen.

"*Hola, Sahar!*" she said cheerfully, passing my bedroom in her bikini top and sarong. "*Would you like a fresh juice?*"

"*Siiiii,*" I replied, practicing the Spanish word I was most comfortable with.

I got out of the white hammock chair, adjusting my Daisy Dukes and bikini top before meeting her in the kitchen.

"*How many bikini's do you have, chica!?*" she exclaimed, as she had almost every day since I got here three weeks ago.

I smiled with my hands on my hips. "*Jou like, jou like?*"

She smiled, *"Let's use all these papayas y limones from the garden."* She gestured with her chin. I took the hint and began to prepare them.

We had gotten into a good groove living together at her new guesthouse.

Just eight months ago, she was the stranger I'd rented a room from on a last-minute solo trip. I'd been escaping Robi. We shared the same birthday, and it was our first one apart. My skin crawled at the thought of staying in New York and celebrating without him. So I found an escape.

I could hear her accent and flare in the e-mail welcoming me to Puerto Rico:

Hola Sahar!

I am leaving the key for you in the mailbox, wrapped in a vintage pink and green silk scarf. Let yourself into the house, hydrate yourself with fresh juice, and try the quinoa salad. There will be beach towels and sarong here for you to use! Un beso—Sofia

I had walked up to a grand wooden door, the smell of incense seeping through its cracks. I pushed it open and was greeted by a pair of boots identical to my own. I immediately felt at home, and the protective walls around me came crumbling down.

Walking upstairs, I found a sticky note with my name on it. On the desk was a Buddha head, a candle, and a burning gardenia incense. I sat down on my bed, took in a huge breath, then laid my forehead into my hands and wept.

Hours later I met Sofia face-to-face for the first time. We stayed up talking for the next 6 hours about love, life, God, yoga, and Ayahuasca.

On the last day of my birthday trip she had driven us to a worn down house and got out.

"What's this?" I asked

"We're here to pick your room," she replied with a mischievous smile.

"Wait! What?! Are you serious?!"

"Siiii Sahar. This is the guesthouse I was telling you about. You have a room if you want to come back and stay here."

I felt like my guardian angel had just swooped me up and gave me the chance to break the cycle of emptiness I was living in back in New York.

"I wouldn't be able to come until April," I said with no hesitation and great certainty.

Sofia was clear with her boundaries from the moment I moved into the Peacock House, and I was too exhausted from New York to do anything but fit into the nooks and crannies of them.

The sounds of the drill started again and a hummingbird escaped into our kitchen where we always had a bowl of honey out for her.

She was beautiful and one of my favorite parts of living in a home that represented everything I wanted to get away from. I often thought how ironic it was to have a budding business, construction, and a revolving door of new people, all in my new home. So much for leaving New York behind. It was the same tempo, with new flavors.

Now Sofia poured my fresh juice and topped it with a basil leaf before toasting my glass. "We have a guest checking out and another checking in today. So, the room and bathroom need to be clean."

I wasn't sure how to respond. *Was she just sharing her responsibilities as the owner, or was she expecting me to help her clean?*

I had been couch surfing in New York to save up for my rent in Puerto Rico, with every expectation that I could just surrender to my exhaustion. I didn't realize when I committed to moving into Sofia's new guesthouse, I was also signing up to work part-time.

Unable to form any words, I nodded in agreement and switched my focus to the tasty benefits of living in the Peacock House.

Then the drilling started again. I tilted my head back and finished the rest of my juice.

"I'm going to la playa. I'll be back."

"Okay. Enjoy." She replied without looking up from her phone.

I walked to my room and slipped out of my shorts, grabbed my sunglasses, keys, and phone. My bare feet made a hushed noise as they shuffled sand along the tile floor. I couldn't help but think of how annoyed Sofia got when the floors were so sandy. *She probably blames me.*

I exhaled and exited the creaky iron gate, ready to break free from the obligation and guilt.

"Thank God I'm here." I mumbled as I took a slow blink, gazing up at the sun and trying to release the overwhelming feeling in my chest and head. I knew all life's solutions started with a talk with Sofia that I had no energy for. I couldn't even think of how to start the conversation.

My long hair tickled my back and brought me back to my almost naked body walking freely down the sidewalk, like I had been doing it all my life. Firmly pushing my ear buds into my ears, I tuned everything out through the only way I knew how to offer myself nurturing: music.

I'm a rebel, soul rebel

I'm a capturer, soul adventurer

See the morning sun

On the hillside

not living good

travel wide

Said I'm a living man

I've got work to do

If you're not happy,

children then you must be blue. (Bob Marley)

THE VOICE OF BOUNDARIES

*T*he pure exhaustion I led myself to in New York didn't leave any energy for me to be fearful of leaving behind all I had built there and starting over in Puerto Rico.

I was prepared to take full advantage of island life: quiet time to rest, ocean sounds to guide my reflection, and plenty of yoga to bring me insight for my next step.

I wasn't expecting that life had another lesson to offer me at a time when I felt utterly burnt out.

My first three months in Puerto Rico, I faced challenge after challenge with Sofia, my health, and men—a trifecta that forced me to find and use my voice. I was 33 and my wisdom would not let me treat myself badly anymore.

Knowing how to get in touch with my inner voice and decipher which parts of me were making decisions is by far the best thing my tumultuous life has gifted me.

At this point in my life, I am where you are:

~ **Aware of my inner voice.**

~ **Able to hear when my voice is expressing healthy or unhealthy emotions.**

~ **Familiar with the change in my voice when she is coping by being dramatic or shushed.**

When I got to Puerto Rico I was fully aware of and disappointed in myself for losing my voice in my relationship with Robi and not using my voice wisely in my career.

I had adopted my abandoned voice and stayed in that relationship out of the fear of being unlovable to another, despite knowing the whole time I was doing myself a disservice.

During that same time I tried my best to adopt a nurturing voice to hold onto any part of my self-esteem by empowering others through Free Your Star. Although it served its purpose for the most part, it ended up emptying me more than serving my bigger purpose.

The voice of boundaries is what I was missing.

I did not draw a line and speak up for what I deserved in my relationship and with my paycheck. This issue followed me to Puerto Rico.

Moving is not change; it's just geography.

Setting boundaries is the most important way to **preserve the voice** you are getting to know.

By not setting boundaries you are repeating your old voice.

You are saying it is still okay to be treated in a way that does your life a disservice.

In Sofia's energy, I went back to the voice I had when my family first moved to the States, feeling like I had to earn my keep. I felt guilty for taking up room in the guesthouse and not participating more in its success.

The reality was that I was a paying tenant who was in the process of rebuilding her entire life—an emotional situation I had been very honest to Sofia about. There were countless opportunities for me to set boundaries, and I was fully aware of them. That's the thing, we usually are.

Can you think of a time you agreed to something and as you were agreeing:
Yeah, I'm free…. sure, no problem…. I don't mind bringing the….

Inside you were saying: *No!…. Sh*t! Why did you agree to that! …. I have such a busy day Friday, I shouldn't have promised!*

We've all done it before.

Take some time to recollect a few experiences where you wanted to (but just didn't) say no, agreed to something you really didn't want to do, or stayed quiet and accepted less than you deserved.

What was the situation where you did not set a boundary?

What kept you from setting this boundary?

What are the costs of not setting this boundary?

What have you avoided in your life because of situations similar to this?

There is this silent expectation that tells us that once we agree to something, whether a date or a pay rate, we have lost our opportunity to change our mind and set a boundary.

I firmly do not believe in this rule.

You have every right to go back and approach a family member, lover, friend, co-worker, or supervisor and say, *You know, I've done some thinking, and I would love to revisit our conversation the other day about…*

People expect you to set boundaries, to stand up for what is right for you. Expect that for yourself from now on.

The more you use this voice, the easier it gets for you and for those who interact with you. When they are invited to speak true to what works for them, people will. This takes away so much miscommunication, and allows an abundance of grace and joy into your experiences.

It's much easier to think of creating "grace" and "joy" by staying quiet and respecting other people's boundaries versus setting your own. Going with the flow. Literally, the story of my life up to this point.

What I didn't realize is that, although it takes a certain assertiveness to set boundaries, it does not have to be a defensive encounter, which is what always made me shy away from setting boundaries.

It's not an argument. It's a conversation.

Working up to a conversation with Sofia took me many, many walks on the beach. Despite her overtaking energy, she had been so nurturing to me, and I wanted to make sure I was aware of her feelings as well as my own.

I practiced the approach, the first line to the conversation, for many days. When I finally did speak to Sofia, I reminded myself that this was my friend. I just needed to be real with her about how I was feeling.

The pressure was lifted, and I allowed myself to be vulnerable in my honesty.

Her demeanor reflected mine—calm and supportive in what I was sharing and my decision to move out. It also made her reflect on the reality she had built for herself by living in her business. She, too, was worn out.

That conversation was healthy for both of our lives and saved a friendship that is one of the dearest and most impactful in my life to this day.

That conversation led me to understand the thought process my voice needs before she speaks aloud her boundaries.

Many of us are not like Sofia. The voice of boundaries is not natural to us.

The idea of setting a boundary becomes much harder than it really is when you blow it up in your head. That's a big part of setting boundaries; it's really a conversation about two perspectives finding a middle ground.

Read on and find which voice of boundary best suits your personality.

Plain n' simple. You are not much of a conversationalist and feel much more comfortable if things are short and sweet. Keep a calm demeanor and don't embellish the information.

~ I really enjoyed hearing about your project, but I can't add more to my schedule right now.

~ The cost of supplies is $15 and my fee is $45.

Sharing is caring. Don't be afraid to disclose to someone how you are feeling. This will lower the intensity of emotions and help diffuse the situation. Sharing about yourself will help both of you know this is not an attack.

~ I'm feeling hurt about last night, and I wanted to chat with you about it.

~ I want to be cool with the news you gave me, but I'm getting anxious and want to talk more about it.

I feel you. You are being aware of the other person's feelings first and foremost, but still sticking to what you need.

~ I understand that you are busy, but I need to know if you can meet the deadline.

~ I know you preferred the other color, and I really appreciate your flexibility to use orange.

Win:Win. Sometimes saying what you want is not enough to make what you need happen. This happens a lot in our romantic relationships. Rather than let the situation deflate you or become a source of future resentment, discuss what both of you need, and agree to disagree.

I know you really want to go to the museum, but I really want to go to the beach. Can we schedule a different day, when the weather is not so nice, to go to the museum, or should we each do our own thing today? What do you think?

Remixed. When your boundary isn't heard the first time, no need to get quiet or snappy, just say it in a new way.

~ You've already told your significant other that you cannot help them on a particular day. You are asked again, and can reply: *No my love, remember that's a really hectic day for me. I can help you tomorrow morning instead. Does that work?*

Saying NO. Set the most effective boundaries with one word: No.

~ Thank you so much for thinking of me, but I'm not going to be able to.

~ I realize this is really important to you. I'm just not up to it. Please understand.

This is the only place in this book where I will ask you to practice the voice you are learning aloud. And perhaps your voice of boundaries will be expressed through writing and not vocally.

Whatever your solution, make sure you keep this voice active for the rest of your life.

She is your birthright.

Setting limits sets you free.

Find the tone of voice that works for you to set boundaries. A few tips…

- Politely ask to talk.

- Use "I" statements; don't attack

- Be aware of what you need from your environment (private place vs. public venue).

- Give facts without judgment. It's okay to say what you need and inquire the same about the other person.

- Stick to your perspective and feelings while being empathetic to the other person.

- Give the other person a chance to voice their opinion. It's a discussion, not an argument.

- Accept that sometimes you agree to disagree.

The voice of guilt or fear may come up for you when it comes to boundaries. They will make you think…

I look selfish.

People won't like me.

She or he will get angry.

I get too nervous to set boundaries.

Give yourself permission.

Bottom line, when you voice boundaries, you are actively forming the life you crave.

Join me at www.FindYourVoice.center for this chapter's yoga and meditation session.

EIGHT

VOICE OF COMPARISON & GUILT

TURNING POINT

SPRING 2013 ~ AURORA, COLORADO ~ MOM'S HOUSE

I had slept in the same position all night. My body was stiff from being pressed into the mattress by the three blankets that cocooned me from the wintery weather.

Why is it so f***ing cold? I woke up annoyed that I was back in Colorado.

Quickly putting on my socks, slippers, and robe before losing any body heat, I shuffled to the bathroom. Reaching under all the layers to find the top of my pants, I nearly peed on my own leg before sitting down on the freezing toilet seat.

Dammit that's cold! I immediately raised to a squat position and ended up peeing on my leg anyway.

I turned on the hot tap and looked at the stream of icy water that initially gushed out, knowing how unpleasant it would feel. The bathroom water always needed time to heat up. My hands found their way to the edges of the sink, bracing my weight. My chin fell into my chest, and I exhaled in defeat.

A tear found its way out of my right eye and down to the corner of my mouth. I used my tongue to catch it from going any further, and my morning breath shook me out of my sadness.

I closed my eyes and slid my hands under the lukewarm water, feeling the slipperiness of the soap between my fingers. I smiled. It reminded me of the slimy pebbles in the river of *El Yunque.*

Damn I'm going to miss that place, ran across my mind. My chest tightened at the thought of how much life had changed in just 24 hours.

The white suds of the toothpaste really made me realize how dark my face was from spending all day in the sun yesterday.

Beach life suits me. I have to find a way to get back.

"Alright, enough!" I said aloud pointing at my reflection, spitting toothpaste all over it.

I had gotten into the habit of talking aloud to all the thoughts that tried to tell me it was a mistake to move back in with my mom. I knew it was something that had to be done.

Inhaling deeply.

I readjusted my attitude before greeting her for our first morning together.

"Salaam azizam!" I said cheerfully, putting forth all effort to bring joy into our morning.

"Well, good morning!" she replied, surprised by my demeanor. "Pour yourself coffee and come tell me all about yourself."

The heat of my coffee cup and the space heater I was standing in front of had no chance against the cold front of my negativity when I looked outside and saw more than a foot of snow.

"ARE YOU SERIOUS!? I can't believe it's snowing like this. This sucks." I said aloud, no energy left to filter my difficulty adjusting to being back home.

"I know baby, but it's good writing weather!" Mom replied with a calm certainty, "Remember what I told you in Puerto Rico. You have a gift, you have every right to use it, and that's why you're here."

She'd been so tender since her trip to visit me in San Juan.

Our first morning together there I'd brought her a cup of coffee in bed, ready to plan our day when she surprised me with a series of questions.

"Tell me everything that happened when you were little," she began.
That question, and my honest answers, totally changed our relationship from estranged mother and daughter to best friends.

A shiver brought me back from my thoughts of Puerto Rico to the cold room.
"You're right, Mama! Thank you for reminding me." I nodded my head and sent a wink her way.

"So, what do you want to eat for dinner?"

I started to chuckle. "Ma! We haven't even eaten breakfast!"

"Welcome home," she replied with a huge smile.

VOICE OF COMPARISON & GUILT

My time in Puerto Rico was delicious, a luxury I do not take for granted. I lived off very little, yet it was a time that enriched my life the most.

Between bartering, small jobs, and my savings, I was able to extend my time there for a year. After I moved out of the Peacock House, Sofia took me to a rustic cabin called *La Finca* in Vieques. It was there that the first words of *Find Your Voice* began to flow out of me.

I'd been in Puerto Rico almost nine months at that point. That entire time I was shedding so many voices, especially the tone I had set my life to in New York. It was a constant battle between my new vision of life and the standards my voice was used to equating with success.

I did not want to shape my life around the expectations of my family just so I could be validated. I also didn't want to keep the pressure of quick success that was instilled in me from the energy of New York.

I was ready to pour love into the details of making my dreams a reality for as long as I needed to. My wisdom told me it would be a long process to write *Find Your Voice* and to be able to sustain my financial security life from it.

For a while, I told myself, *You can always get a desk job if you need to.*

This gave me comfort when the voice of anxiety spoke up. It reminded me that I have other capabilities that will not leave me homeless or without food (survival mode is my second nature that leads to desperate decisions, a voice I have to be very aware of).

My true voice was beginning to step into her full power and would remind me: *You have no choice but to go for it. This is what you are meant to do. This will serve the greater good.*

This clarity, being able to hear the most powerful voice within me and not push her down, talk her out of her ideas, or shy away from her vision, was the most powerful learning point in my process.

It allowed me to realize I had to commit to a daily change to achieve what I wanted.

Once I accepted this, I stopped comparing my timeline to others' and really respected my process.

I was not drained by the fact that every day I was committing my time, energy, and money to something only I understood and believed in. I accepted that my priorities as a woman had changed, and this would reflect in all areas of my life.

I had to consistently give myself permission to write, to be in the moment with my wisdom, and trust that I was smart enough to make a living from it once I had the book "out of me."

I was constantly fighting against going back to survival mode and looking for a job, and I did take jobs. But every time I would accept more responsibility and stray away from what my true voice was telling me, I would get sick or depressed.

The process of living true to my voice was constantly rebutted by thoughts that were now "bilingual":

How will you make any money? You don't have a husband supporting you.

Really, NOW you're going to be a writer, estupida? You're no Elizabeth Gilbert.

Now, tu familia is definitely going to think you're full of stupid decisions, loca, loca, loca.

Okay, first you will have to get a website, then you will have to get articles published, then...

The voice of comparison and my true voice had daily battles. It was exhausting.

Being back in Colorado literally felt like I was taking a step—a decade-long leap—backwards. I was approaching my mid-thirties; while my friends were having kids, I was making my mom's linen closet into my shoe closet.

The voice of comparison made me feel a lot of regret for my past decisions. She took me all the way back to high school, comparing my decisions to those of my friend, who now owns a house on a golf course.

I neglected the fact that we had entirely different backgrounds, resources, and, most important, personalities. I would die of boredom from her life. No house is big enough to hold that much regret.

That's the thing: comparisons are usually unfair.

We take the worst about ourselves against the best **image** of others.
You have no idea what that other person's process includes or if it would feel good for you. **You just assume. Be careful.**

When you compare, you are spending your energy on someone else's life.

Find your true voice; stop this thought process as soon as it starts.

You will naturally compare yourself to others. It's a part of digesting the world around you.

The goal of finding your voice is never to hush these voices.

It's to keep making decisions from your true voice, *despite* these voices.

You have nothing to gain from the voice of comparison. **You only lose when you compare.** You lose the authenticity of who you are by highlighting what someone else has experienced.

I'm going to take you back into the different areas of your life with the voice of comparison in mind.

Give yourself permission to be honest.

These are little moments that you repeat, at times without knowing. This voice will make you feel bad. You have a choice to not make an idol of your comparisons. Accept where you are in your process. You have the capability to get you what you want!

Lifestyle:

Who/ what do you focus your comparison on?

What from this comparison do you want in your life?

What capability do you have to gain the same for yourself?

How does this comparison serve you? What feelings does it bring out in you?

How do you want to feel in this area of your life? *(Not what do you want to own or do, but feel.)*

What do you do well in this area of your life?

How can you give yourself permission to accept what you have in this part of your life?

Body & Wellness:

Who/ what do you focus your comparison on?

What from this comparison do you want in your life?

What capability do you have to gain the same for yourself?

How does this comparison serve you? What feelings does it bring out in you?

How do you want to feel in this area of your life? *(Not what do you want to own or do, but feel.)*

What do you do well in this area of your life?

How can you give yourself permission to accept what you have in this part of your life?

Creativity & Learning:

Who/ what do you focus your comparison on?

What from this comparison do you want in your life?

What capability do you have to gain the same for yourself?

How does this comparison serve you? What feelings does it bring out in you?

How do you want to feel in this area of your life? *(Not what do you want to own or do, but feel.)*

What do you do well in this area of your life?

How can you give yourself permission to accept what you have in this part of your life?

Relationship & Society:

Who/ what do you focus your comparison on?

What from this comparison do you want in your life?

What capability do you have to gain the same for yourself?

How does this comparison serve you? What feelings does it bring out in you?

How do you want to feel in this area of your life? *(Not what do you want to own or do, but feel.)*

What do you do well in this area of your life?

How can you give yourself permission to accept what you have in this part of your life?

Spirituality:

Who/ what do you focus your comparison on?

What from this comparison do you want in your life?

What capability do you have to gain the same for yourself?

How does this comparison serve you? What feelings does it bring out in you?

How do you want to feel in this area of your life? *(Not what do you want to own or do, but feel.)*

What do you do well in this area of your life?

How can you give yourself permission to accept what you have in this part of your life?

I hope you were able to keep it real with yourself.

Remember, these pages are a safe place for the heavy stuff.

Don't judge yourself. There is enough in this world that works against you; no need to join the posse.

You have the power to be your own healer.

You have a voice and a process that is only your own.
There will always be someone with more or who is better.
But there is never a voice, a vision, like yours. There is a way about you that no one else has. A way of seeing the world that adds to it.

By giving your true voice a way to express herself, you are offering others in your energy the space to do the same. It's infectious.

That's what fueled me to write this book.
The vision of one woman at a time stepping into her power, whatever that looks like.

She then becomes another example of a woman living true to her voice, words, and wisdom. I envision us all holding hands, forming a wave of nurturing that will heal what our patriarchal society has done to our most authentic power.

It's not about putting down a man. It's about embracing the womanly voice in you.

Preserve your voice. Hear her out immediately.

When you hear the destructive voice of comparison arise, listen.

Your first reaction will be to push her away; instead, recognize what she wants from the situation. Take on a nurturing voice and see what she is craving.

See her perspective without putting yourself down.

Denying the voice of comparison will make her talk resentment, and she will talk you into feeling like a failure. Give her room to feel, and she will not rule over your perspective.

Sh*t will happen to challenge this balance between comparison and your true voice.

You are going to be challenged by situations out of your control in life. If you are experiencing personal illness, relationship problems, family illness, financial difficulties, or just sleeping problems, you will not be yourself and you'll wish for another's circumstance.

Take on your nurturing voice for a little **self-therapy** in these times. Here are a few questions to help guide yourself when you are down:

What is my voice of comparison saying?

Am I honestly representing myself in this situation?

What positive gain did I make recently that I did not account for?

What voice am I taking to cope / resolve the situation?

Did I overreact?

Is there any other perspective I can see about this situation?

What am I feeling?

Reflect on your progress.
Remind yourself often of your growth.

Preserve the voice you have gotten to know by not comparing her to another. Accept responsibility without shame when you mess up. Don't compare your process to another's.

When you prepare yourself to grow—your voice, your career, your home—you will deal with missteps, comparison, and guilt.

As women, it's rare for us to set aside time and effort to invest in ourselves without guilt. Whether it's an hour to work out or read or to make plans that don't include your family members, it is rare for us to set those boundaries without feeling bad about it.

There is also a certain guilt that comes when you begin to flourish into the best version of you while those around you are in a different process. Change is difficult for people. Your ability to operate from your true voice will allow you to make more decisions that offer you a very fulfilling life.

Sometimes this process is just as difficult for you as it is for those around you, especially if they are in a negative rut of their own.

Lead by example.

Do not feel bad for setting boundaries.

Do not feel guilty for wanting more for yourself.

Do not feel that you are being arrogant when you recognize your power.

Do not feel bad when you are the smartest or most engaging in the room.

Be empathetic to others and respect that you can only do so much for their process.

Do not feel bad when all eyes are on you. Enjoy the attention, and be willing to reciprocate.

As you're growing, there will be lists, goals, and setbacks. Just as finishing this book was a goal for you at one point. If you are finishing it thinking you should have done more... STOP.

Respect your process.

You <u>have the tools</u> to work through the layers and hear your most powerful voice. You can trust that you will make decisions from your wisest voice as you continue to grow.

With every challenge…
…setting boundaries,
…negotiating a salary,
…becoming a wife or a mother,
…taking the leap and starting your own business,

… your voice will be tested.

Let go of the guilt you assign yourself by immediately taking action to counter it. Otherwise the voice of guilt will…

Affect your self-esteem.

Prevent you from moving forward.

Speak a lot of self-criticism that will make you obsess over perfection.

Apologize often by saying, "I'm sorry" for even the most insignificant things.

Adopt the voice of paranoia and often think that others view you as inadequate.

The ongoing voice of guilt can lead to heaviness in your chest, anxiety, and depression.

The voice of guilt is one that I deal with quite a bit.

When you are closed and do everything yourself, there is a huge guilt that comes with accepting help or even asking for it. Being vulnerable enough to accept help is one of the biggest catalysts to any change, including finding your voice.

Through the process of writing and publishing this book, I was ultra aware of my voice of guilt when it came to my mom's support.

It was a beautiful experience to receive it, but I had to also work on taking in her emotional and financial support without feeling bad about it. This took many conversations between her and myself about the voice I had grown into.

It is difficult for many of us to *receive*, and I will tell you that is the first way you are keeping yourself from growing.

You don't have to do it alone.

You are deserving of someone's understanding, time, and resources.
The more you give to yourself, the more you can give to your family, friends, and community.

Use your voice to converse.
Words have a beautiful healing power.
You have gotten to know the words and voices within you.
Trust them to guide conversations that will heal and add meaning to any area of your life.

Learn to forgive yourself and others.

Make space for permission in your life.

Stumble, jump, fall, leap, and use your voice to share it with others.

Above all else, rejoice that you have the voice of a woman in this day and age where we have a choice to use our voice to **create the world we want to exist in.**

A beautiful place to practice dealing with the voice of comparison and guilt is on the yoga mat. This time, I'm going to suggest you invite a friend over or go to a class.

What the person is doing next to you is none of your business. You will want to compare yourself to your neighbor or feel guilty for not spending more time working out or drinking more water. This is the time when you go back to your breath. Go back to the reminder that you are exactly where you need to be in your process. Set an intention before class, maybe a word for your inhale, and another for your exhale or a phrase that will keep your mind at ease.

One of the biggest resources I had during my turning point was my spiritual support system. The feeling of trusting yourself is much like the practice of putting trust in something intangible.

I hope that you have been involving your beliefs, whatever they are, with the process of finding your voice.

You were created with a voice of your own and your creator can help you get in touch with it.

Visit www.FindYourVoice.center for this chapter's meditation.

NINE

THE VOICE OF RECOGNITION

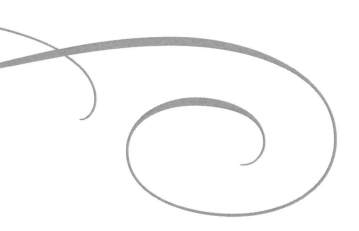

I'M THE SHERO OF THIS STORY.

PRESENT DAY...

*Y*ou've read my story. When I was the victim and the victor.

We've spoken about my process and layers of coming into my voice.

The story for this chapter does not belong to my voice. The hero -the shero- of this story is you.

I want to make permanent in your perspective what you have learned in this process.

Finding your voice can sometimes be difficult to recognize when you are in the thick of it.

You will be revisited by some of the emotions you started with, and that's when I want you to have this particular experience to refer to. The story that belongs to **your process** while reading and working with these pages.

You've gotten to know the voice within you.
You've recorded her. Reflected on how she feels and copes.
Her emotions. Her opinions. Her strengths. Her permissions. Her triggers.
You've been offered the tool kit to become the shero of your story.
Recognize that.

I offer you this space to have some fun with expressing where you were when you picked up this book and where you are now.

You can describe the actual location and the emotions that you held.
You can focus just on who you were leading up to finding your voice.
You can just use words, or just doodle stick figures.

Let this be a space for reflection of growth, change, transformation...

A new awareness.

Don't get overwhelmed by the details. Remember what you learned in chapter one, think and detach. Be the author or filmmaker of this storyboard.

Think of it as describing your experience of two different memories.

Two separate experiences, stepping stones... voices.

People & Places

Situation

Thoughts &
Emotions

People & Places

Situation

Thoughts &
Emotions

People & Places

Situation

Thoughts &
Emotions

People & Places

Situation

Thoughts &
Emotions

People & Places

Situation

Thoughts &
Emotions

People & Places

Situation

Thoughts &
Emotions

THE VOICE OF RECOGNITION

I hope that you were able to express what you have learned since picking up this book.

There was a set of questions in chapter 1 that revealed to you how ready you were to commit to finding your voice.

Your ability to express your story at the beginning of this chapter, to recognize the difference between when you started and now, gives you great insight into how you are able to recognize your efforts.

The voice of recognition is the ultimate healer.

She will offer you the apology and empathy you never got.
She will see the small changes and remind you how big they are.
She will understand your struggle and have your back when no one else will.
She will have empathy for your process and agree with you when it sucks.

The fact that your eyes have met this page is a great accomplishment.

The timeline and struggle of getting here is not the focus. The celebration comes from your commitment to listen, feel, and take action to invest in your life. Your voice.

Honor this space of validation and you will build a space so safe, so secure and nurturing within yourself that it will withstand the volatile world.

Take some time to reflect on efforts, changes, or transformations that you've noticed. I'm providing you with all the different areas of life, but don't feel that you need to have a recognition for all of them. Fill out what applies. These pages will be here for you as you continue your process.

Lifestyle

Body & Wellness

Creativity & Learning

Relationship & Society

Spirituality

By bringing the voice of recognition into your life, you will never feel the need to prove anything.

This voice is what held me together during the entire process of writing and publishing this book.

Those close to me voiced their fear about me sharing so honestly.
Close friends told me that I needed to be perfect before putting myself out there.
I even had a family member voice my worst fears aloud, confirming my whispers that I was a loser for living at home *at my age,* and of all things, being a writer.

Sure, these things hurt, swayed my emotions, and sometimes served as constructive criticism.

My voice of recognition validated the emotions I was processing as a result of digesting these interactions.

She also recognized the work I had put in that no one else saw or understood. She was the voice that soothed my anxiety.

She is such an important voice, that even if you close this book and forget everything else, I ask you to just remember the voice of recognition.

She will keep you grounded and remind you of what you have already accomplished and, most importantly, what you are capable of.

The only way you will not reach your potential, live the life you crave, is if **your** voice gets in the way.

The voice you came to find through these pages has been with you this whole time.

She was sad, timid, anxious, or confused.

You've heard her and learned how she copes.

You've learned to detach from her destructive side.

Your emotions and actions will now follow your lead.

Enjoy this beautiful dance with your authentic voice.

Let her lead you to the life you've always wanted.

Trust that she will help you get out of your own way when you need to speak up.

Be aware of the emotions that stop you from taking action, from getting vocal.

Recognize you've unlocked the source that blocks your courage...

Your own voice.

You know how to listen to her and detach from her when she thinks of things or brings up emotions that don't serve you.

This relationship you now have with your voice will always give you the option to choose courage over the thoughts floating in your head. Detach your worth from these judgments.

Respect the process of battling this same cycle.

Don't get lazy and stop putting in the work.

Make this a lifestyle change.

You will see that the anxiety, depression, and loneliness will leave you faster and faster with each go-around.

~I am proud of you.

~Thank you for investing in your voice.

~I need someone like you to exist. So does my future daughter.

~Stay true to your voice, allow it room to waver and be imperfect.

~Set an example to society of how to live with empathy for yourself and others.

~Respect what your emotions have to teach you.

~Always, always choose the perspective of love.

You are already the shero of your story.

ACKNOWLEDGEMENTS

*S*oulseye, I thanked you many times while writing this book. What you taught me about my writer's voice will never be forgotten. There is always a space of deep gratitude within my heart for you.

To my Houston fam-bam (even if you live in Austin now) ~ being in your energy that is nothing but supportive of me and my voice allowed me the safe space to let this book flow from me. I am eternally grateful for all of you and love you more than I could ever express.

Leann Garms ~ you believed in me before you even met me face-to-face. Thank you for helping me keep my voice authentic and offering me the guidance and support to make this book a reality.

Bridget Boland ~ you have served as my soul's compass. Thank you for helping me to stop producing and start singing. I will forever think of you with deep gratitude.

Jeniffer, Brit, Alita and Julio at Monkey C Media ~ your creative translation of my mission brought tears to my eyes on many occasions. I am so fortunate that your voices are a part of this book. I can't wait to create with you all again.

Carmela Nazareno ~ My hype woman, thank you for going on this ride with me as FYV transformed to what it is today. Your generosity of your talent, support and love will never be forgotten.

Jessica Ashcraft ~ See what you've done! Thank you for keeping me in your thoughts and serving as an angel here on earth looking out for me.

Katy Hansel~My dearest mentor, the generosity of your wisdom means the world to me. Thank you for taking the time and energy to invest in a person you barely knew. Your dedication will never be forgotten.

Jessica Stephenson~My first Find Your Voice muse, thank you for taking a chance on me and being so courageous in the journey of finding your own voice. I am so proud of you.

Sarah Prudhomme~Thank you for believing in my voice from the beginning. Your support and fashionable eye are food for the soul!

Lynda Zelenka~My spiritual mentor, thank you for never judging me. Your voice in our community is one that I look up to. God has blessed me with your voice, and I do not take it for granted.

To My Holy Yoga ladies~I am 110% sure that this process was greatly fueled by your prayers. I feel your support to this day and it fills me with joy that my journey includes all of you. I love you girls!

To the voices telling me I was making a big mistake by taking this path, I honor the lesson you brought me. With the last words of this book, let it be written that the words of another have no power over the purpose of the soul.

ABOUT THE AUTHOR

Sahar Paz, a native of Iran was labeled "Bomb Keeper" and "Terrorist" by her classmates at age 9. Her journey from fleeing Iran to the USA, finding success only to have it slip away is one of courage and triumph. Although the bombings in Iran ceased in her life in 1986, the shame and prejudice followed her, creating a war-of-words within that took her to her death bed in 2005. Sahar's mission is to free every woman from her own mental slavery. Through *Find Your Voice* and its accompanying coaching program, she guides women to step into their full power by embracing their most authentic voice.

Today, Sahar is a survivor and change master, dedicated to transforming the lives of teens and women through her work as a speaker, author, yoga instructor and life coach. Sahar's first love is dance. She enjoys the arts and spending time with her family in Houston, where she resides with her dog, Rico.

For information on her speaking, coaching programs, or public appearances:
www.saharpaz.com